Introduction

This workbook is designed to be used in conjunction with "The Essentials of Edexcel Maths – Linear Specification A (1387): Foundation Tier". It is matched page for page to this revision guide and consists of structured questions with spaces for answers, plus extension questions.

The contributors to this workbook are former or current GCSE examiners who have drawn on their experience to produce interesting and challenging exam-style questions, which are designed to reinforce understanding of the material that is covered in the specification.

Details of our other Edexcel Maths Revision Guides and Workbooks can be found on the inside back cover.

The answers to the questions in this workbook can be obtained from the address on the facing page for £1.00 plus 50p postage and packing.

Consultant Editor:

John Proctor B.Sc. (Hons), Cert. Ed.
Director of Specialist College,
St. Mary's Catholic High School,
Astley,
Manchester
(An 11-18 Specialist Mathematics and Computing College)

Proofreader:

Kay Chawner
Formerly a mathematics teacher
at The Ridgeway School, Swindon.

*Although this workbook is intended for candidates following the linear specification, it can also be used by candidates following the MODULAR B (1388) specification.

Contents

Place Value

1 Complete the following table. The first row has been done for you.

Place Value of Digits					Number
10 000 Ten Thousands	**1 000** Thousands	**100** Hundreds	**10** Tens	**1** Units	
		3	2	6	Three hundred and twenty six
a)	5	3	0	7	....
b) 7	3	1	5	8	....
c)		....	....	....	Five hundred and sixty
d)	1	....	....	7	.... , two hundred and forty ....
e)	....	....	....	....	Fourteen thousand and fifty two

2 Round 493 507 to the nearest…

    a) 10 000 ....   **b)** 1 000 ....   **c)** 100 ....   **d)** 10 ....

3 Round 109 109 to the nearest…

    a) 10 000 ....   **b)** 1 000 ....   **c)** 100 ....   **d)** 10 ....

4 If the attendance at a football match was 32 000 to the nearest thousand, what is the lowest possible number and the highest possible number of people that could have attended the match?

    Lowest possible number: ....   Highest possible number: ....

5 The number of boys who attended school on a particular day was 440 to the nearest ten. On the same day the number of girls who attended school was 460 to the nearest ten.

    a) What is the lowest possible difference between the number of boys and the number of girls who attended school on that day? ....

    ....

    b) What is the highest possible difference between the number of boys and the number of girls who attended? ....

    ....

---

6 Draw a table to show the place value of each digit in the following numbers:
    a) one   **b)** eighty seven   **c)** four hundred and nine
    d) six thousand, two hundred and twenty three   **e)** fifty thousand and five

7 Round 30 715 to the nearest...
    a) thousand   **b)** hundred   **c)** ten

Numbers 1 & 2

1 **Here are eight numbers:**

(3) (4) (6) (7) (11) (15) (20) (21)

a) Which three numbers are even numbers? ....

b) Which two numbers are factors of 40? ....

c) Which two numbers are factors of 45? ....

d) Which four numbers are factors of 42? ....

e) Which two numbers are multiples of 7? ....

f) Which three numbers are multiples of 2? ....

g) Which odd number is a multiple of 5 and 3? ....

h) Which number has an odd number of factors? ....

2 **Here are ten numbers:**

(5) (8) (11) (19) (22) (24) (31) (36) (47) (81)

a) Which six numbers are odd numbers? ....

b) Which three numbers are factors of 72? ....

c) Which three numbers are factors of 110? ....

d) Which three numbers are multiples of 3? ....

e) Which three numbers are multiples of 4? ....

f) Which numbers have one and themselves as their only factors? ....

g) Which two numbers have an odd number of factors? ....

3 **What is the reciprocal of…**

a) 8? .... b) 25? .... c) 0.5? .... d) $\dfrac{3}{4}$? ....

4 **The reciprocal of a number is 0.1. What is the number?** ....

5 **Complete the multiplication table below by multiplying the numbers in the first column by the numbers in the top row. The first one has been done for you.**

x	5	7	10
2	10		
3			
4			
5			
6			
7			
8			
9			
10			

Lonsdale REVISION GUIDES   Revision Guide Reference: Page 5 & 6   NUMBER   5

6 Solve the following without using a calculator. Show all your working.

a)
```
   475
 +  28
 _____
```

b)
```
  23179
 + 4830
 _____
```

c)
```
   238
 -  99
 _____
```

d)
```
  43008
 - 1559
 _____
```

e)
```
   423
 x  36
 _____
```

f)
```
  4705
 x   91
 _____
```

g) 16 ⟌ 608

h) 13 ⟌ 3341

i) 41 x 100

j) 573 x 1000

k) 423 ÷ 10

l) 8 ÷ 1000

7 a) A whole number is multiplied by 1 000 giving an answer of 234 000.
What is the number? ....

b) A whole number is divided by 100 giving an answer of 0.08.
What is the number? ....

8 a) The number 864 900 is divided by a power of 10 to give the answer 8.649.
What is the power of 10 used?

....

b) The number 763 is multiplied by a power of 10 to give the answer 76 300 000.
What is the power of 10 used?

....

9 Solve the following without using a calculator. Show all your working.
a) 3 001 + 999 **b)** 4 735 + 381 + 49 **c)** 4 079 - 497 **d)** 13 574 - 9 281 **e)** 473 x 67 **f)** 375 x 413
g) 4 037 ÷ 11 **h)** 47 748 ÷ 23 **i)** 940 x 10 **j)** 403 x 100 **k)** 11 x 1 000 **l)** 33 942 x 10 000
m) 408 ÷ 10 **n)** 55 ÷ 100 **o)** 6 ÷ 100 **p)** 33 942 ÷ 10 000

10 A whole number is multiplied by a certain power of 10 giving an answer of 23 000. When the whole number is divided by the same power of 10 the answer is 2.3.
a) What is the whole number being used? **b)** What is the power of 10 being used?

Integers 1 & 2

1 **a)** Put the following integers into ascending order (lowest to highest):

14, -3, -1, 5, 12, -7, -11, 2

....

b) Put the following integers into descending order (highest to lowest):

-230, 467, 165, -62, -162, 70, -320, 8

....

2 **Complete the following boxes:**

a) **i)** $1 - 3 + \boxed{} = 6$ **ii)** $6 + \boxed{} = 2$ **iii)** $-6 + \boxed{} = -11$

    iv) $-4 - \boxed{} = -9$ **v)** $4 - \boxed{} = -4$ **vi)** $-3 - \boxed{} = 5$

    vii) $-6 \times \boxed{} = 12$ **viii)** $5 \times \boxed{} = -20$ **ix)** $-6 \times \boxed{} = 6$

    x) $-12 \div \boxed{} = -2$ **xi)** $36 \div \boxed{} = -9$ **xii)** $-45 \div \boxed{} = 9$

b) **i)** $-4 - 6 + \boxed{} = 2$ **ii)** $6 - \boxed{} - 3 = 11$ **iii)** $-8 - 3 - \boxed{} = 5$

    iv) $\boxed{} + 2 - 5 = -9$ **v)** $14 - 1 + \boxed{} = -15$ **vi)** $4 - 11 + \boxed{} = -5$

c) **i)** $\dfrac{-6 + \boxed{}}{-3} = 7$ **ii)** $\dfrac{-6 + 2 - \boxed{}}{-5} = 4$ **iii)** $\dfrac{\boxed{} - 6 - 3}{-1} = 4$

    iv) $\dfrac{-3 \times -5 \times \boxed{}}{-6} = 10$ **v)** $\dfrac{9 \times \boxed{} \times -2}{4 - 6} = 9$

d) **i)** $\boxed{} + \boxed{} = -4$ **ii)** $\boxed{} - \boxed{} = -3$ **iii)** $\boxed{} \times \boxed{} = -18$

    iv) $\boxed{} \div \boxed{} = -10$ **v)** $\boxed{} \times -5 \times \boxed{} = 30$

3 **Complete the following boxes by inserting =, +, −, x or ÷ to connect the numbers:**

a) $6 \boxed{} 9 \boxed{} -3$ **b)** $2 \boxed{} 3 \boxed{} -7 \boxed{} 12$

c) $9 \boxed{} 1 \boxed{} -3 \boxed{} -3$ **d)** $-50 \boxed{} 10 \boxed{} 5 \boxed{} 0$

e) $6 \boxed{} -3 \boxed{} 10 \boxed{} 19 \boxed{} 1$

f) $10 \boxed{} -2 \boxed{} 6 \boxed{} 2 \boxed{} 0$

Integers 1 & 2 (cont)

4 The following table shows the highest temperatures (in °C) for eight places on a particular day:

Place	Athens	Berlin	Cairo	Cardiff	London	Madrid	Moscow	New York
Temperature	15	-2	25	2	6	13	-6	18

a) What is the difference in temperature between the following places:

i) Athens and Berlin?...

ii) Cairo and Moscow? ....

iii) Berlin and Moscow?..

b) The next day the temperature in Cardiff had fallen by 2°C and the temperature in Moscow had fallen by 5°C. What was the difference between Cardiff and Moscow?

....

5 Below is part of a bank statement:

LONSDALE BUILDING SOCIETY

Date	Description	Deposit	Withdrawal	Balance
11/12/03				£226.30
12/12/03	The Toy Shop		-£49.99	£176.31
13/12/03	Gas Bill		-£21.03	£155.28
13/12/03	Cheque	£25.00		£180.28
16/12/03	La Trattoria		-£32.98	☐
19/12/03	Rent		☐	-£112.70

a) What was the balance on 16/12/03 after the withdrawal of £32.98?

....

b) On 19/12/03 there was a withdrawal to pay for rent. How much was the withdrawal?

....

6 Put the following integers into ascending order:
   3, -3, -11, 0, 4, 19, -36, 74, -1, 100

7 Complete the following:
   a) 6 – 8 =   **b)** -4 – 4 =   **c)** -1 – 1 + 2 =   **d)** -5 x – 6 x 10 =   **e)** -5 x 3 x 6 =   **f)** -15 ÷ 3 x -4 =   **g)** 100 ÷ 4 x -1 =

8 Complete the following boxes:
   a) ☐ – 3 = 12   **b)** -8 – ☐ = 3   **c)** -6 + ☐ – 2 = 11   **d)** -14 + 20 + ☐ = -10   **e)** ☐ + 4 – 8 = -15

Order of Operations

1 **Calculate the following:**

a) $7 + 5 \times 2$

b) $14 \times 5 - 3$

c) $6^2 + 4 \times 2$

d) $\dfrac{15}{3} + 6$

e) $18 \times 2 - 5^2$

f) $\dfrac{30}{6} - \dfrac{40}{10}$

g) $2^3 + 4^3 \times 3$

h) $6 \times 7 - 10 \times 3 + 8$

i) $15 - 3 \times 6 \times 2 + 5$

2 **a)** Put brackets in the following expression so that its value is 43:

$13 - 3 \times 4 + 3$

b) Put brackets in the following expression so that its value is -8:

$13 - 3 \times 4 + 3$

c) Put brackets in the following expression so that its value is 70:

$13 - 3 \times 4 + 3$

d) Put brackets in the following expression so that its value is 4:

$13 - 3 \times 4 + 3$

e) Put brackets in the following expression so that its value is 20.5:

$3 \times 1.4 + 4 \times 2.5$

f) Put brackets in the following expression so that its value is 12.12:

$7 + 3.2 \times 6 - 4.4$

3 **Calculate the following:**
a) $4 + 3 \times 13$ **b)** $4 \times 3 - 13$ **c)** $4 - 3 \times 13$ **d)** $4^2 \div 2 + 3$ **e)** $9 + 15 \div 5$ **f)** $4 + 7 \times 3 - 15$
g) $14 \div 4 - 5$ **h)** $3 + 7 - 5 \times 3^2$

4 **Put brackets in the following expression so that its value is...** **a)** -1 **b)** 35 **c)** -51

$3^2 - 4 \times 5 + 10$

5 **Put brackets in the following expression so that its value is...** **a)** 54 **b)** -2 **c)** 6

$4^2 - 3 \times 4 + 2$

Rounding Numbers 1 & 2

1 **Round …**

a) 7.321 to **i)** 1 decimal place .... **ii)** 2 decimal places ....

b) 16.781 to **i)** 1 decimal place .... **ii)** 2 decimal places ....

c) 0.01765 to **i)** 2 decimal places .... **ii)** 3 decimal places ....

d) 0.1053 to **i)** 1 decimal place .... **ii)** 3 decimal places ....

e) 7.0707 to **i)** 1 decimal place .... **ii)** 2 decimal places ....

2 **Dave weighs 68.4kg to 1 decimal place. What is the lowest measurement and the highest measurement possible for his actual weight to 2 decimal places?**

Lowest possible weight: .... Highest possible weight..............................

3 **Helen's height is 1.65m to 2 decimal places. What is the lowest measurement and the highest measurement possible for her actual height to 2 decimal places?**

Lowest possible height: .... Highest possible height..............................

4 **Round...**

a) 432 to **i)** 1 significant figure .... **ii)** 2 significant figures ....

b) 9 154 to **i)** 1 significant figure .... **ii)** 2 significant figures ....

c) 10 047 to **i)** 2 significant figures .... **ii)** 4 significant figures ....

d) 0.0238 to **i)** 1 significant figure.............................. **ii)** 2 significant figures ....

e) 0.0001736 to **i)** 2 significant figures.............................. **ii)** 3 significant figures ....

f) 0.010366 to **i)** 2 significant figures .... **ii)** 3 significant figures ....

5 **The attendance at a pop concert was 5 700 to 2 significant figures. What is the difference between the lowest possible actual attendance and the highest possible actual attendance?**

....

....

---

6 **Round 135.6742 to a)** 1 decimal place **b)** 2 decimal places **c)** 1 significant figure
d) 2 significant figures **e)** 3 significant figures

7 **Round 0.06038 to a)** 1 decimal place **b)** 2 decimal places **c)** 3 decimal places
d) 1 significant figure **e)** 2 significant figures **f)** 3 significant figures

8 **Fran's weight to 1 decimal place is 47.6kg. What is the difference between her highest possible weight and her lowest possible weight to 2 decimal places?**

9 **a)** Use your calculator to work out the value of $(1.46)^2 \times 6.71$. Write down all the digits on your display.
b) Round your answer to a suitable degree of accuracy.

Estimating and Checking

1 **a) i)** Work out 106 x 53 using a calculator ....

ii) Without using a calculator check your answer by estimation.

....

b) i) Work out 3.8 x 15.2 using a calculator ....

ii) Without using a calculator check your answer by estimation.

....

c) i) Work out $\dfrac{29.4 \times 5.8}{19.6}$ using a calculator ....

ii) Without using a calculator check your answer by estimation.

....

d) i) Work out 384 x 7.1 using a calculator   ....

ii) Without using a calculator check your answer by estimation.

....

2 **John and Donna collect and keep all their loose change. The table below shows how much they collected for three successive months.**

MONTH	JOHN	DONNA
JUNE	£7.36	£9.10
JULY	£8.90	£16.58
AUGUST	£13.47	£4.52

a) John has calculated that he has collected £29.73 altogether.

i) Check by estimation whether this is likely to be correct.

....

ii) Check John's calculation for accuracy.

....

b) Donna has calculated that she has collected £31.20 altogether.

i) Check by estimation whether she is likely to be correct.

....

ii) Check Donna's calculation for accuracy.

....

....

3 **Check the following calculations by estimation and then for accuracy. Finish by making any necessary corrections.**
a) 13 + 29 + 43 = 82 **b)** 9.06 + 11.58 + 7.23 + 13.86 = 41.73
c) (3 x 6.25) + 92 − 10 = 101.75 **d)** (4.7 x 6.3) + (0.8 x 9.5) = 40.21

Powers and Roots

1 **Work out the value of...**

a) 2^3 .... b) 3^2 .... c) 4^3 ....

d) 10^3 .... e) 5^3 .... f) 6^2 ....

2 **Here are ten numbers:**

$$10 \quad 18 \quad 25 \quad 27 \quad 45 \quad 64 \quad 80 \quad 125 \quad 133 \quad 196$$

a) Which three numbers are square numbers? ....

b) Which three numbers are cube numbers? ....

c) Which one of these numbers is a square number and a cube number? ....

d) Which of the above numbers is equal to 4^3? ....

3 **Work out the value of...**

a) $\sqrt{25}$ .... b) $\sqrt{9}$ .... c) $\sqrt{144}$ ....

d) $\sqrt{121}$ .... e) $\sqrt{49}$ .... f) 4^3 ....

g) 5^3 .... h) 6^3 .... i) 7^3 ....

4 **Here are ten numbers:**

$$2 \quad 4 \quad 5 \quad 8 \quad 10 \quad 20 \quad 27 \quad 36 \quad 64 \quad 80$$

a) Which three numbers have an integer square root? ....

b) Which three numbers have an integer cube root? ....

c) Which one of these numbers has an integer square root and an integer cube root? ....

5 **Work out the value of...**

a) 10^2 .... b) 10^3 .... c) 10^4 ....

d) 10^5 .... e) 10^6 .... f) 10^7 ....

6 **Work out the value of...**

a) 4^3 b) 4^1 c) $4^3 \times 4^1$ d) $4^3 + 5^2$ e) $8^2 + 3^3$ f) $6^2 - 3^2$

g) $\dfrac{8^2}{2^2}$ h) $\dfrac{3^3 - 7}{2^2}$ i) $10^2 + 3^3 + 5$

1 Here are eight fractions:

$$\frac{35}{50} \ , \ \frac{16}{40} \ , \ \frac{60}{90} \ , \ \frac{28}{40} \ , \ \frac{30}{40} \ , \ \frac{40}{100} \ , \ \frac{84}{120} \ , \ \frac{10}{25}$$

a) Which three fractions are equivalent to $\frac{2}{5}$? ....

b) Which three fractions are equivalent to $\frac{7}{10}$? ....

2 Express the following fractions in their simplest form:

a) $\frac{27}{30}$ ....

b) $\frac{42}{6}$ ....

c) $\frac{84}{105}$ ....

d) $\frac{108}{184}$ ....

3 a) Arrange the following fractions in ascending (lowest to highest) order:

$$\frac{5}{6} \ , \quad \frac{3}{5} \ , \quad \frac{11}{15} \ , \quad \frac{2}{3} \ , \quad \frac{1}{2}$$

....

b) Arrange the following fractions in descending (highest to lowest) order:

$$\frac{9}{40} \ , \quad \frac{3}{5} \ , \quad \frac{5}{8} \ , \quad \frac{9}{10} \ , \quad \frac{1}{4}$$

....

4 Write down two fractions that are greater than $\frac{7}{10}$ but less than $\frac{5}{6}$.

....

5 a) Write the following improper fractions as mixed numbers:

i) $\frac{11}{5}$ ....

ii) $\frac{13}{6}$ ....

iii) $\frac{24}{5}$ ....

iv) $\frac{32}{3}$ ....

b) Write the following mixed numbers as improper fractions

i) $3\frac{1}{3}$ ....

ii) $5\frac{1}{4}$ ....

iii) $11\frac{3}{5}$ ....

iv) $20\frac{1}{20}$ ....

---

6 Write down three fractions that are equivalent to each of the following:

a) $\frac{2}{3}$ **b)** $\frac{4}{7}$ **c)** $\frac{9}{11}$

7 Express the following fractions in their simplest form and then arrange then into ascending order:

$$\frac{28}{35} \ , \quad \frac{38}{40} \ , \quad \frac{75}{100} \ , \quad \frac{42}{84} \ , \quad \frac{99}{110}$$

8 Write down three fractions that are greater than $\frac{4}{5}$ but less than $\frac{9}{10}$.

Fractions 3

1 Solve the following additions and subtractions without using a calculator. Show all your working and give your answers in their simplest form.

a) $\dfrac{3}{4} + \dfrac{2}{3}$

b) $\dfrac{2}{9} + \dfrac{7}{8}$

c) $4\dfrac{1}{2} + 2\dfrac{9}{10}$

d) $7\dfrac{5}{8} + 4\dfrac{1}{3}$

e) $\dfrac{9}{10} - \dfrac{1}{2}$

f) $\dfrac{13}{15} - \dfrac{2}{3}$

g) $4\dfrac{4}{5} - 1\dfrac{3}{8}$

h) $9\dfrac{1}{6} - 4\dfrac{3}{5}$

2 At a football match the crowd is made up as follows:

$\dfrac{5}{12}$ of the crowd are over 40 years old, $\dfrac{1}{4}$ of the crowd is between 20 years old and 40 years old, and the remainder of the crowd is less than 20 years old.

What fraction of the crowd is less than 20 years old? Give your answer in its simplest form.

....

....

....

....

3 Solve the following multiplications and divisions without using a calculator. Show all your working and give your answers in their simplest form.

a) $\dfrac{1}{4} \times \dfrac{2}{5}$

b) $\dfrac{9}{10} \times \dfrac{2}{7}$

c) $\dfrac{3}{4} \div \dfrac{9}{10}$

d) $\dfrac{7}{8} \div \dfrac{7}{12}$

e) $\dfrac{1}{2} \times \dfrac{3}{5}$

f) $\dfrac{1}{4} \times \dfrac{5}{7}$

g) $\dfrac{1}{2} \div \dfrac{2}{3}$

h) $\dfrac{1}{2} \div \dfrac{1}{4}$

i) $\dfrac{8}{9} \times 4$

j) $\dfrac{7}{10} \div 3$

4 Solve the following without using a calculator. Show all your working.

a) $\dfrac{7}{10} + \dfrac{5}{8}$ b) $2\dfrac{1}{3} + 4\dfrac{3}{8}$ c) $\dfrac{9}{10} - \dfrac{2}{3}$ d) $4\dfrac{1}{2} - 3\dfrac{7}{10}$ e) $\dfrac{2}{5} \times \dfrac{7}{10}$ f) $\dfrac{13}{15} \div \dfrac{4}{5}$

g) $4\dfrac{1}{2} \times 5$ h) $2\dfrac{1}{3} \div 6$

Calculations Involving Fractions

1 James wants to buy a CD player costing £240.

As a deposit he pays $\frac{1}{8}$ of the cost. How much deposit did James pay?

....

....

2 Mary buys a new car costing £13 000.

As a deposit she pays $\frac{2}{5}$ of the cost. The remainder she pays monthly over a period of 4 years.

a) How much deposit does Mary pay?

....

....

b) What is her monthly repayment if she pays the same amount each month?

....

....

c) At the end of the 4 years Mary decides to sell her car. It is now worth £7150. Express its value now, after 4 years, as a fraction of its value when new. Give your answer in the simplest form.

....

....

3 A shop holds a sale where all items are reduced by $\frac{1}{6}$.

a) Calculate the sale price of an item which cost £93.60 before the sale.

....

....

....

b) The sale price of another item is £121.50. Calculate its price before it was reduced.

....

....

....

4 A football match lasts $1\frac{1}{2}$ hours. During the match the ball is out of play for a total of 15 minutes. Express the total length of time that the ball is in play as a fraction of the time that the match lasts. Give your answer in its simplest form.

5 In a sale, a washing machine has its original price reduced by $\frac{1}{2}$. The following week the sale price is further reduced by $\frac{1}{4}$.

a) If the washing machine originally cost £600, calculate its sale price after **i)** the first reduction, **ii)** the second reduction.
b) If the washing machine costs £150 after both reductions what was its original price?

6 Express 40 seconds as a fraction of 1 hour.

Decimals 1 & 2

1 Complete the following table (the first row has been done for you).

	Place Value of Digits							Decimal Number
	100 Hundreds	10 Tens	1 Units	DECIMAL POINT	$\frac{1}{10}$ Tenths	$\frac{1}{100}$ Hundredths	$\frac{1}{1000}$ Thousandths	
			3	•	4	2		3.42
a)	1	0	2		5			....
b)		1	3		4	7	1	....
c)			....		....	....	....	8.407
d)		9	0		0	3	1	....
e)	....	....	....		....	....	....	423.008

2 Use a calculator to write the following fractions as either recurring or terminating decimals, to four decimal places.

a) $\frac{2}{3}$ ....

b) $\frac{2}{5}$ ....

c) $\frac{1}{11}$ ....

d) $\frac{7}{9}$ ....

3 Arrange the following decimals in ascending order of value:

$$6.3, \ 0.36, \ 3.6, \ 0.306, \ 0.63$$

....

4 Complete the following additions and subtractions without using a calculator. Show all your working.

a) 13.62 + 7.77   b) 103.2 + 4.837   c) 40.75 − 8.29   d) 723.4 − 6.19

---

5 Write the following fractions as decimals, to four decimal places.

a) $\frac{3}{8}$ b) $\frac{2}{9}$ c) $\frac{1}{30}$ d) $\frac{22}{25}$ e) $\frac{4}{15}$

6 Arrange the following decimals in descending (highest to lowest) order:
14.32, 1.432, 143.2, 13.42, 14.23, 1.342

7 Mrs Green goes shopping. She buys four tins of baked beans at 37p each, 3 tins of spaghetti at 29p each and 2 boxes of cornflakes at £1.37 each. She pays for her goods with a £10 note. How much change does she receive?

8 Peter puts three boxes in the boot of his car. They weigh 8.4kg, 6.73kg and 13.03kg. What is the total weight of the load?

Multiplication of Decimals

1 Solve the following without using a calculator. Where possible show all your working.

a) 4.7 x 10   **b)** 13.246 x 10   **c)** 0.00146 x 100   **d)** 136.3 x 1 000

....

e) 7.56 x 13   **f)** 4.72 x 2.3

g) 16.56 x 17.3   **h)** 4.713 x 1.56

2 If 27 x 36 = 972 write down, without making any further calculations, the value of...

a) 2.7 x 36   ....   **b)** 27 x 0.36   ....   **c)** 2.7 x 3.6   ....

d) 0.027 x 36   ....   **e)** 0.27 x 0.36   ....

3 If 231 x 847 = 195 657 write down, without making any further calculations, the value of...

a) 0.231 x 847   ....   **b)** 231 x 84 700   ....

c) 0.231 x 847 000   ....   **d)** 2 310 x 8.47   ....

4 Solve the following without using a calculator.
Where possible show all your working.
a) 15.67 x 10   **b)** 0.0101 x 100   **c)** 3.4671 x 1000   **d)** 2.32 x 11
e) 4.67 x 1.8   **f)** 146.2 x 2.45   **g)** 13.33 x 0.23   **h)** 9.4 x 0.003

5 If 3.52 x 4.7 = 16.544 write down, without making any further
calculations, the value of...
a) 352 x 47   **b)** 3.52 x 47   **c)** 0.352 x 4.7   **d)** 3.52 x 0.047

6 A school holds a raffle. The three prizes cost £24.65, £17.99 and
£9.89. 130 tickets were sold at £1.25 each.
How much profit did the school make from the raffle?

7 Jim is going to hire a cement mixer. The cost is £24.50 for the
first day and £3.75 for each extra day. Jim wants to hire it for 7
days. How much will it cost him in total?

8 A shirt costs £24.95. How much is this in euros if £1 = €1.60?

£24.95

Division of Decimals

1 Solve the following without using a calculator. Where possible show all your working.

a) 16.3 ÷ 10   b) 0.347 ÷ 10   c) 14 632.4 ÷ 100   d) 1.2467 ÷ 1 000

....

e) 37.6 ÷ 8   f) 41.04 ÷ 1.2

g) 1 141.72 ÷ 0.23   h) 549.6 ÷ 1.2

2 If 72.8 ÷ 56 = 1.3 write down, without making any further calculations, the value of...

a) 72.8 ÷ 5.6 ....   b) 7.28 ÷ 56 ....   c) 72.8 ÷ 0.56 ....

d) 0.728 ÷ 56 ....   e) 728 ÷ 56 ....

3 If 27 x 34 = 918 write down, without making any further calculations, the value of...

a) 918 ÷ 27 ....   b) 918 ÷ 3.4 ....   c) 91.8 ÷ 27 ....

d) 9.18 ÷ 3.4 ....   e) 91.8 ÷ 340 ....

---

4 Solve the following without using a calculator. Where possible show all your working.
a) 7.162 ÷ 10   b) 0.0034 ÷ 100   c) 473.1 ÷ 1 000   d) 707.4 ÷ 9   e) 24.64 ÷ 1.4   f) 0.08788 ÷ 0.0013

5 If 58.82 ÷ 3.4 = 17.3 write down, without making any further calculations, the value of...
a) 58.82 ÷ 0.34   b) 5 882 ÷ 0.34   c) 58.82 ÷ 17.3   d) 3.4 x 17.3

6 A school holds a raffle. The three prizes cost £9.49, £14.99 and £19.99. Tickets cost 75p each. What is the minimum number of tickets that need to be sold for the school to make a profit?

7 Jean is going to hire a wallpaper stripper. The cost is £8.50 for the first day and £1.25 for each extra day. When she returns the wallpaper stripper the total hire charge is £24.75. For how many days did she hire the wallpaper stripper?

Percentages 1

1 **Calculate the following amounts:**

   a) 20% of 60p

   b) 30% of 6.5km

   ....

   ....

2 **Express ...**

   a) £18 as a percentage of £90

   b) 42cm as a percentage of 8.4m

   ....

   ....

3 **Alan has kept a record of his height and weight from when he was age 10 and age 16.**

Age 10	1.2m tall	40kg weight
Age 16	1.74m tall	64kg weight

   a) i) Calculate the increase in his height from age 10 to age 16 ....

   ii) Express this increase as a percentage of his height at age 10.

   ....

   ....

   b) i) Calculate the increase in his weight from age 10 to age 16 ....

   ii) Express this increase as a percentage of his weight at age 10.

   ....

4 **A train ticket costs £17.60 when bought on the day of travel. If the same ticket is bought in advance it costs £15.40. Express the saving you make when you buy the ticket in advance as a percentage of the full ticket price when bought on the day of travel.**

   ....

   ....

   ....

5 **Calculate the following amounts:**
   a) 45% of £2.60, **b)** 80% of 6.4kg, **c)** 5% of £10.40.

6 **a)** Express 46cm as a percentage of 69cm, **b)** Express 200m as a percentage of 200km,
   c) Express 550g as a percentage of 2kg.

7 A tin of tomato soup weighs 420g. Special tins weigh 546g. Calculate the increase in the weight of a special tin as a percentage of the weight of a normal tin.

8 A brand new car bought in the UK costs £18 000. The same car bought abroad costs £14 850. Calculate the decrease in the price when the car is bought abroad as a percentage of its price in the UK.

Percentages 2

1 A brand new car costs £15 000. It is estimated that it will depreciate in value by 23% in the first year. What is the value of the car at the end of the first year?

....

....

2 The average attendance at a football club over a season was 32 500. In the next season there was a 6% increase in the average attendance. What was the average attendance for that season?

....

....

3 Mr and Mrs Smith bought a house for £120 000. Each year since the value of the property has appreciated by 10%.

a) Calculate the value of the house 2 years after they bought it.

....

....

b) What would the value of the property be after 2 years if the rate of increase was 5%?

....

....

4 **Jim buys a new motorbike for £10 000. a)** If the value of the motorbike decreases by 20% each year, calculate the value of the motorbike after three years.

....

....

b) Calculate the value after three years if the rate of decrease was 10% per annum.

....

....

5 An electrical shop has a sale. All items are reduced by 20%. The following week the shop takes 10% off its sale prices. Pat wants to buy a fridge that was priced at £100 before the sale. She reckons that she will save 30% of this price and that the fridge will now cost her £70. Is she correct? Explain why.

6 A bottle of ink weighs 220g. Calculate the weight of a bottle which is $12\frac{1}{2}$% heavier?

Percentages 3

1 Phil has been told by his mum that he needs to spend 1 hour a day doing his homework, an increase of 50%. How long did Phil originally spend doing his homework each day?

2 An electrical shop has a sale. All items are reduced by 15%. A tumble drier has a sale price of £122.40. What was the price of the tumble drier before the sale?

3 A man buys an antique clock. He later sells it for £5 040, an increase of 12% on the price he paid for it. How much did the clock cost him?

4 Dave is a long distance lorry driver. On Tuesday he drives 253km. This is a 15% increase on the distance he drove the previous day. How far did he drive on Monday?

5 Jean has her house valued. It is worth £84 000. This is a 40% increase on the price she originally paid for it. How much did Jean pay for her house?

6 A clothes shop has a sale. All prices are reduced by 30%. The sale price of a dress is £86.80. What was the original price of the dress?

7 Mrs Smith buys some shares. In twelve months their value has increased by 15% to £3 680. How much did she pay for the shares?

8 Mr Jones collects stamps. After two years he has increased the number of stamps in his collection by 120% to 660. How many stamps did he have in his collection two years ago?

Converting Between Systems

1 Complete the following table. The first row has been done for you.

	Fraction (simplest form)	Decimal	Percentage
	$\frac{1}{2}$	0.5	50%
a)	$\frac{3}{10}$		
b)		0.45	
c)			37.5%
d)	$\frac{2}{3}$		
e)		0.125	
f)			84%
g)	$1\frac{4}{5}$		
h)		4.6	
i)			225%

2 $\frac{3}{5}$ of the CDs in Peter's collection are pop music. Is this more or less than 55% of his collection? Explain your answer.

....

....

3 **a)** Write the following fractions and percentages as decimals:

i) $\frac{2}{5}$ .... **ii)** 35% .... **iii)** $\frac{1}{3}$ .... **iv)** 44% ....

b) Write these numbers in ascending order.

$$44\%, \quad \frac{2}{5}, \quad 35\%, \quad 0.42, \quad \frac{1}{3}, \quad 0.25$$

....

....

4 **a)** Write the following as decimals: **i)** $\frac{4}{5}$ **ii)** 90% **iii)** $\frac{17}{20}$ **iv)** 85%

b) Write these numbers in descending order: $\frac{19}{20}$, 0.75, 90%, 0.92, $\frac{4}{5}$, 85%

5 **a)** Write the following as percentages: **i)** 0.62 **ii)** $\frac{3}{5}$ **iii)** 0.56 **iv)** $\frac{29}{50}$

b) Write the following numbers in ascending order: 61%, $\frac{3}{5}$, 0.56, 0.62, $\frac{29}{50}$, 65%

Everyday Maths 1 & 2

1 **a)** Alma buys a washing machine. The price is £380 + VAT at 17.5%.

How much does the washing machine cost in total?

....

....

b) The total cost of a home stereo system is £517 including VAT at 17.5%.

What is the price of the home stereo system before VAT?

....

....

2 **Mr Smith wants to invest £20 000 for 4 years. He has two options:**

SIMPLE INTEREST AT 5% PER ANNUM OR £7 000 AT THE END OF 4 YEARS

a) Which option will make him the most money? Show all your working.

....

....

....

b) After a further 3 years, with both options, he gets an additional
bonus of £2 000. Which option is better now? Show all your working.

....

....

....

....

....

....

....

....

3 **Peter wants to buy a car. There are two payment options:**

Cash price: £8 000 or hire purchase: 30% deposit + 24 monthly payments of £255

a) What is the deposit required for hire purchase?

....

b) Calculate the percentage increase if Peter pays for the car by hire purchase compared to buying the
car at the cash price.

....

....

....

4 Mr Spark receives an electricity bill. Complete the bill by filling in the gaps.

Meter Reading				Amount (£)
Present	Previous	Units Used	Pence per unit	
32467	30277	i) _____	8p	ii) _____
			Quarterly charge	9.60
		Total charged this quarter excluding VAT		iii) _____
			VAT at 5%	iv) _____
			Total payable	v) _____

5 Use the timetable alongside to answer the following questions:

a) Grace wants to arrive in London before midday. What is the latest train she can catch from Millford station to get there in time and how long will her train journey take?

_____

_____

b) Simon needs to get to Woking by 11.15am because he has a job interview. What is the time of the last train he can catch from Farncombe?

_____

c) What percentage of trains departing from Woking station take less than 30 minutes to arrive at London Waterloo?

_____

_____

Petersfield, Millford, Farncombe, Woking to London Waterloo

Mondays to Fridays

	AN	NW	AN	AN	AN
Petersfield	0752	0811	0833	0901	0928
Liphook	—	—	—	—	—
Haslemere	—	—	—	—	—
Witley	—	—	—	—	—
Millford (Surrey)	0806	0829	0845	0917	0941
Godalming	—	—	—	—	—
Farncombe	0822	0850	0900	0937	0959
Guildford	—	—	—	—	—
Reading	—	—	—	—	—
Woking	0830	0900	0907	0947	1007
Heathrow Airport (T1)	—	—	—	—	—
Clapham Junction	—	—	—	—	—
London Waterloo	0903	0932	0939	1018	1036

Mondays to Fridays

	AN	NW	AN	AN	AN
Petersfield	0949	0956	1019	1049	1055
Liphook	—	—	—	—	—
Haslemere	—	—	—	—	—
Witley	—	—	—	—	—
Millford (Surrey)	1002	1011	1032	1102	1114
Godalming	—	—	—	—	—
Farncombe	1017	1032	1047	1117	1132
Guildford	—	—	—	—	—
Reading	—	—	—	—	—
Woking	1026	1043	1059	1128	1142
Heathrow Airport (T1)	—	—	—	—	—
Clapham Junction	—	—	—	—	—
London Waterloo	1052	1111	1125	1155	1211

6 What is the total cost of a vacuum cleaner if the price is £180 + VAT at 17.5%?

7 Mr Brum wants to buy a car costing £6 000. He buys it on hire purchase paying £124 a month for 3 years. His total repayment is £6 264. What percentage deposit did he pay?

8 Mr Plug receives an electricity bill. The cost per unit is 8p and the quarterly charge is £9.60. It says on his bill that the total payable for this quarter excluding VAT is £80.24. How many units has he used this quarter?

9 Using the timetable above, what is the difference between the average journey time of Peak time trains and the average journey time of Off Peak trains travelling from Petersfield to London Waterloo? Trains that arrive at London Waterloo after 10am are classified as Off Peak.

Ratio & Proportion 1 & 2

1 **Jim weighs 70kg. His sister Cathy weighs 35kg.**

a) Calculate the ratio of Jim's weight to Cathy's weight.

....

b) Express your answer to part a) in the form 1:n ....

2 **Freya is 90cm tall. Her brother Tom is 1.35m tall.**

a) Calculate the ratio of Freya's height to Tom's height.

....

b) Express your answer to part a) in the form 1:n ....

3 $\frac{3}{7}$ **of the teachers at a school are male.** **a)** What is the ratio of male teachers to female teachers?

....

b) Express your answer to part a) in the form 1:n ....

4 **A large tin of baked beans costs 36p and weighs 450g. A small tin of baked beans costs 22p and weighs 250g.**

a) Calculate the ratio of the weight of the two tins ....

b) Calculate the ratio of the cost of the two tins..

c) Which tin represents the best value for money? Explain your choice.

....

....

5 **a)** Divide 80p in the ratio of 2:3   **b)** Divide 6m 30cm in the ratio 2:3:4

6 **£5 000 is shared between three women in the ratio of their ages. Their combined age is 120 years. If Susan gets £2 500, Janet gets £1 500 and Polly gets the remainder, what are their ages?**

....

....

....

....

7 In a maths class there are 30 pupils on the register and the ratio of girls to boys is 3:2. If 4 girls and 2 boys are absent from the class what does the ratio of girls to boys become?

....
....
....
....
....
....

8 A builder makes concrete by mixing cement, gravel, sand and water in the ratio 2:8:5:3 by weight. How many kilograms of sand, to the nearest kg, does he need to make 10 000kg of concrete?

....
....
....
....
....
....

9 **Opposite is a recipe for making 10 biscuits.**

a) Calculate the amount of each ingredient needed to make 25 biscuits.

....
....
....
....

Recipe
90g of flour
130g oatmeal
80g margarine

b) How many biscuits can be made using 0.715kg of oatmeal?

....
....
....
....

---

10 **100ml of semi skimmed milk contains 4.8g carbohydrate and 1.8g fat.**
a) What is the ratio of carbohydrate to fat? **b)** Express your answer to part a) in the form 1:n

11 **A large tub of margarine weighs 500g and costs £1.10. A small tub of margarine which normally weighs 250g has an extra 10% free and costs 52p. Which tub of margarine represents the best value for money? Explain.**

12 **Divide …**
a) 4.2cm in the ratio 1:2, **b)** 980g in the ratio 2:3:4:5

13 **450 tickets were sold for a raffle at 20p each. The ratio of the cost of prizes to profit made is 5:13. How much profit did the raffle make?**

14 **The angles of a quadrilateral are in the ratio 2:3:5:8. What is the size of the largest angle?**

15 **A large packet of washing powder weighs 2.5kg and costs £5.60. How much should a 750g packet of washing powder cost if it represents the same value as the large packet?**

The Basics of Algebra

1 **Simplify…**

a) $a + 2a$

b) $3a - 2a$

c) $5x + 6x$

d) $11x - 4x$

e) $11a - 6a$

f) $15p - p$

g) $9p - 2p + 4p$

h) $11p + 5p - 12p$

i) $2a^2 + 3a^2$

j) $5b^2 + 6b^2$

k) $10w^2 - w^2 + 2w^2$

l) $11a^2 - 5a^2 - 12a^2$

m) $2a + 3b + 4a + 5b$

n) $8a + 3b + 4a + 8b$

o) $7c - 8d - 9c + 10d$

p) $11c - 4d - 6c + 9d$

q) $3a \times 2b$

r) $6c \times 6d$

s) $12pq \times 2r$

t) $4ab \times 5c$

u) $4ab + 8cd - 7ab + cd + ab$

v) $11cd + 4dc - 3cd$

w) $-4x^2 + 6x + 7 + 3x^2 - 11x + 2$

x) $6ab + 4cd - 2ba + 7dc$

y) $14 - 8p^2 + 11p + 2p^2 - 4p + 3$

z) $4ab^2 + 6a^2b - 3ab^2 - 5a^2b$

2 **Explain why $2x + 3x = 5x$ is an example of an identity and not an equation.**

3 **Simplify…**

a) $12x + 6x$ b) $12x - 6x$ c) $12x \times 6x$ d) $12x \div 6x$ e) $4p^2 - 11p^2$

f) $19ab - 13bc + 2ab + 16bc$ g) $13ab + 4a^2b - 2ab^2 + 3a^2b - 4ab + 10ab^2$

Substitution

1 **If p = 2, q = 5 and r = -4, find the value of ...**

a) $2p + 3q$ ....

b) $2(p + q)$ ....

c) $2pq$ ....

d) p^2q ....

e) $pq - q^2$ ....

f) pqr ....

g) $p^3 + r^2$ ....

h) $\dfrac{4p}{r}$ ....

i) $p^2q^2 + \dfrac{r}{p}$ ....

j) $\dfrac{p}{q} + \dfrac{r}{q}$ ....

2 **If $x = \frac{1}{2}$, $y = \frac{1}{3}$ and z = -2, find the value of ...**

a) $x + y$ ....

b) xz ....

c) xz^2 ....

d) $\dfrac{1}{x} + z$ ....

3 **Find the value of ...**

a) $3x - 7$ when $x = -3$ ....

b) $4(x^2 - 1)$ when $x = -3$ ....

c) $4(x-1)^2$ when $x = 5$ ....

d) $(x + 2)(x - 3)$ when $x = 6$ ....

e) $(x^2 - 5)(x + 8)$ when $x = -5$ ....

4 **If e = 3, f = 8, g = -4 and h = $\frac{1}{4}$, find the value of ...**
   a) ef **b)** fg **c)** gh **d)** $e + f + g$ **e)** $f + g + h$ **f)** $e^2 - f$ **g)** g^2h **h)** $f \div g$ **i)** $e^3 + g$ **j)** $2f \div g^2$ **k)** $\frac{1}{e} + h$ **l)** $e^2 + f + g^2$

5 **Find the value of ...**
   a) $5x^2 - 3$ when $x = -4$ **b)** $5(x - 3)$ when $x = -4$ **c)** $5x^2 - 3$ when $x = -2$ **d)** $(x + 3)(2x - 1)$ when $x = 2$
   e) $(x^2 + 3)(x - 5)$ when $x = -1$

Brackets and Factorisation

1 **Expand and simplify ...**

a) $4(2x + 1)$

b) $3(3r - 7)$

c) $2(3m + 2)$

d) $11(4 - 3x)$

e) $5(4x - 3y)$

f) $4(3 + p)$

g) $x(5 + 3x)$

h) $10(4x - 3)$

i) $x(4 - x)$

j) $5(-4 + x)$

k) $-3(2 + x)$

l) $3(-2 + 4p)$

m) $2p(4 - p)$

n) $6r(r - 3)$

o) $10x(4x - 3)$

p) $5(2y + 4) + 3$

q) $5(2 - 3x) + 7x$

r) $11(5 - 3x) - 9$

s) $10(3x - 4) - 9x$

t) $5(3 - 2x) + 7$

u) $4x(2x + 3) + 5x$

2 **Factorise the following expressions:**

a) $5x + 10$

b) $4x - 8$

c) $6x + 10y$

d) $5x^2 + 7x$

e) $8p + 13p^2$

f) $4a^2 - 5a$

g) $20ab + 5cd$

h) $10ab - 15bc$

i) $10x^2 + 5x$

3 **Expand and simplify ...**
   a) $6(4x - y)$ **b)** $3x(2x + 5)$ **c)** $4x^2(2y - x)$ **d)** $6x(3 - x^2)$

4 **Factorise the following expressions:**
   a) $9x - 15$ **b)** $9x + 9$ **c)** $20x^2 - x$ **d)** $4x - 20x^3$

Solving Linear Equations 1 & 2

1 **Solve the following equations:**

a) $5x = 35$

b) $3x + 4 = 16$

c) $5x + 8 = 23$

d) $4x - 7 = 5$

e) $10x - 8 = 12$

f) $8 + 3x = 29$

g) $2(x + 2) = 12$

h) $5(x - 3) = 10$

i) $4(5 + 3x) = 14$

j) $5x = 2x + 9$

k) $7x = 15 - 3x$

l) $2x = x - 8$

m) $11x + 3 = 3x + 7$

n) $5 + 7x = 23 + 3x$

o) $10x - 6 = 3x + 15$

p) $8(3x - 2) = 20$

q) $5(x + 7) = 3(9 + x)$

r) $8(4x - 6) = 7(3x - 10)$

2 **a)** Joan thinks of a number.

If you multiply it by 3 and add 12 the answer is 27.

Let the number Joan thinks of be x.

Form an equation and solve it.

b) Jim thinks of a number.

If you divide it by 4 and then add 11 the answer is 13.

Let the number Jim thinks of be x.

Form an equation and solve it.

Solving Linear Equations 1 & 2

3 **Maggie is x years old.**   **Nigel is twice Maggie's age.**   **Helen is 4 years older than Nigel.**

a) Write down an expression in terms of x for their combined age.

....
....
....

b) Their total combined age is 64 years. Form an equation and solve it to find Helen's age.

....
....
....

4 ABC is a triangle:

a) Write down an expression in terms of x for the perimeter of the triangle.

....
....

b) The perimeter of triangle ABC is 50cm. Form an equation and solve it to find x.

....
....
....

5 ABCD is a rectangle:

a) Write down an expression in terms of x for the area of the rectangle

....
....

b) The area of rectangle ABCD is 72cm². Form an equation and solve it to find x.

....
....
....

---

6 **Solve the following equations to find the value of x:**
a) $2x + 5 = 17$ b) $15 + 3x = 3$ c) $4x = x + 18$ d) $10x = 7x - 15$ e) $4x - 3 = 6x + 12$ f) $9x + 7 = 4x - 13$
g) $14 + 5x = 7x + 2$ h) $23 - 8x = x - 4$ i) $40x - 36 = 7x + 30$ j) $4(x + 5) = 36$ k) $7(2x - 3) = 14$ l) $6 = 4(3x - 9)$
m) $16 = 4(11 - 5x)$ n) $5(x + 1) = 2(x + 7)$ o) $11(3x + 2) = (6x - 5)$ p) $9(2x + 4) - 4(5x + 8) = 0$

7 **Janice thinks of a number. If you subtract 6 from it and then multiply by 3 the answer is 21.**
Let the number that Janice thinks of be x. Form an equation and solve it to find the value of x.

8 **For each of the following form an equation and solve it to find x.**
a)   b)   c)

Formulae 1 & 2

1 **Rearrange the following formulae to make x the subject:**

a) $x + 4y = 3$

....

....

b) $6x + 7y = 50$

....

....

c) $7x - 5 = 3y$

....

....

d) $6y = 10 - 3x$

....

....

e) $x + 3y = 20$

....

....

....

f) $4x - 3 = 8y$

....

....

....

g) $5x + 3y = 3(6 - x)$

....

....

....

....

h) $4x - 5 = 3y$

....

....

....

i) $5x - 6y = 0$

....

....

....

....

j) $5x + 3 = 7y$

....

....

....

....

2 **The circumference of a circle is given by the formula 2πr. Calculate the circumference of the circle alongside if the radius is 4cm and π = 3.14.**

....

....

....

....

....

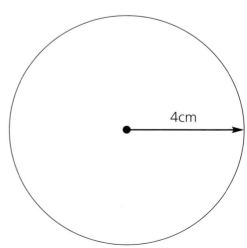

4cm

Formulae 1 & 2 (cont)

3 The distance travelled (s) by an object depends on its initial speed (u), its final speed (v) and the time of travel (t). It is given by the formula:

$$s = \left(\frac{u + v}{2}\right) t$$

Calculate the distance travelled in metres if initial speed = 4m/s, final speed = 12m/s and time = 5.5s

....

....

4 The formula that converts a temperature reading from degrees Celsius (°C) into degrees Fahrenheit (°F) is:

$$F = \frac{9}{5} C + 32$$

What is the temperature in degrees Fahrenheit if the temperature in degrees Celsius is 50°C?

....

....

....

5 The area of a circle is given by the formula $A = \pi r^2$.

a) If π = 3.14, calculate the area of a circle, which has a radius of 5cm in cm².

....

....

....

b) If π = 3.14, use the above formula to work out the area of a circle, which has a radius of 40cm in cm². Give your answer to two significant figures.

....

6 Rearrange the following formulae to make p the subject:
a) $4p - 3 = 4q$ **b)** $4 - 6p = q$ **c)** $3(2p + 5) = 4p + 11q$

7 The area of a parallelogram is given by the formula: Area = length x height. Calculate the area, in m², of a parallelogram that has length = 90cm and height = 1.2m.

8 A garden centre buys shrubs at wholesale prices. They calculate the sale price (s), at which they are sold to customers, by increasing the wholesale price (w) by 50% and adding £2.50 per shrub.
a) Generate a formula for calculating the sale price of a shrub. **b)** If the wholesale price of a shrub is £4.00, use your formula to calculate its sale price.

Number Patterns & Sequences

1 **a)** The first four numbers of a sequence are:

1, 3, 7, 15...

The rule to continue this sequence of numbers is:

**Multiply the previous
number by 2 and
then add 1**

i) What are the next two numbers in the sequence?

....

ii) The following sequence obeys the same rule:

-2, -3, -5, -9...

What are the next two numbers in this sequence?

....

b) The first four numbers of a sequence are:

3, 4, 6, 10...

The rule to continue this sequence of numbers is:

**Subtract 1 from the
previous number and
then multiply by 2**

i) What are the next two numbers in the sequence?

....

ii) The following sequence obeys the same rule:

1, 0, -2, -6...

What are the next two numbers in this sequence?

....

2 **a)** The first four square numbers are 1, 4, 9 and 16. What are the next four numbers in the sequence?

....

b) The first three cube numbers are 1, 8 and 27. What are the next two numbers in the sequence?

....

3 **Here is a sequence of diagrams made up of squares:**

Diagram 1   **Diagram 2**   **Diagram 3**   **Diagram 4**

**The rule for the number of squares is that
each diagram has four more squares in it
than the previous diagram.**

a) How many squares would there be in Diagram 5?

....

b) Which number diagram would have 29 squares?

....

4 **Draw the next two diagrams of the following sequences:**

a)   **b)**

Plotting Points

1 Write down the coordinates of all the plotted points below.

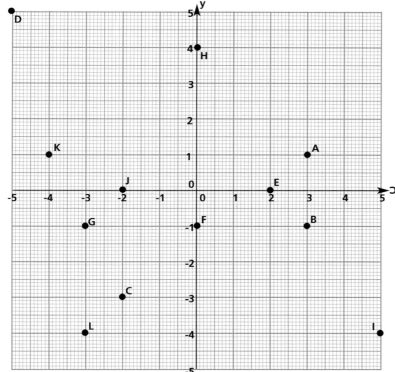

A (.................... , ...)

B (.................... , ...)

C (.................... , ...)

D (.................... , ...)

E (.................... , ...)

F (.................... , ...)

G (.................... , ...)

H (.................... , ...)

I (.................... , ...)

J (.................... , ...)

K (.................... , ...)

L (.................... , ...)

2 Use the axes below to help you answer the following questions:

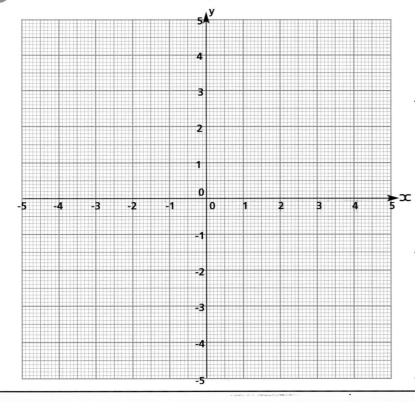

a) The coordinates of 3 points are A (3,0), B (0,-3), C (-3,0). What are the coordinates of point D if ABCD is a square?

....

b) The coordinates of 3 points are P (4,2), Q (3,-2), R (-2,-2). What are the coordinates of point S if PQRS is a parallelogram?

....

c) The coordinates of 3 points are E (1,5), F (4,4), G (1,-3). What are the coordinates of point H if EFGH is a kite?

....

3 The coordinates of 3 points are A (2,3), B (2,-2), C (-3,-2). What are the coordinates of point D if ABCD is a square?

4 The coordinates of 3 points are P (-4,0), Q (3,4), R (4,0). What are the coordinates of point S if PQRS is a kite?

Graphs of Linear Functions 1 & 2

1 On the axes provided, draw and label the graphs of the following linear functions for values of x between -2 and 2:

a) $y = 2x$

x	-2	0	2
y	-4	0	4

b) $y = 2x - 1$

x	-2	0	2
y	-5		

c) $y = x + 2$

x			
y			

d) $y = -2x$

x			
y			

e) $y = -x - 3$

x			
y			

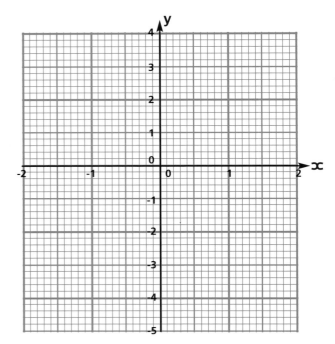

2 On the axes provided, draw and label the graph of the linear function $y = x + 3$, for values of x between -2 and 2.

x			
y			

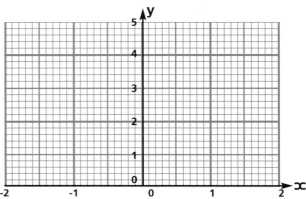

3 On the axes provided, draw and label the graph of the linear function $y = -x + 4$ for values of x between -2 and 2.

x			
y			

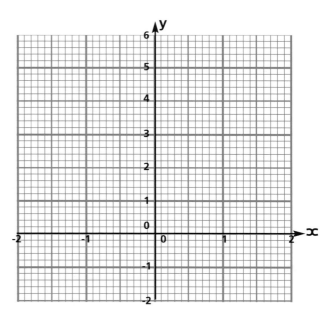

4 On graph paper, plot the graphs of the following linear functions for values of x between -2 and 2:
a) $y - 3x = 1$ **b)** $y - 2x = 7$ **c)** $y - 4x = -6$

1 Two towns A and B are 100 miles apart.
Mr Brown lives in A and drives to B,
Mr Smith lives in B and drives to A, on the
same day, along the same route.
Using the graph opposite...

a) What time did Mr Smith set off?

....

b) Which motorist completed the journey in
the shortest time? ....

c) Who reached the highest speed and what was it? ....

d) What happened at Y? ....

e) Who stopped and for how long? ....

2 Here is part of a travel graph of Tina's
journey to the shops and back.

a) Calculate Tina's speed in km/h for the first
20 mins...

....

b) Tina spends 20 mins at the shops, then
travels back home at 48km/h.
Complete her journey on the graph.

....

3 a) Plot the following data onto this velocity-time graph.

Time (s)	0	1	2	3	4	5	6
Velocity (m/s)	0	5	10	15	20	20	25

b) Between what times was the object travelling at a
steady velocity or speed?

....

....

4 A train leaves town A for town B at 1pm and maintains a steady speed of 60km/h. At 2pm another train leaves
B for A maintaining a speed of 72km/h. The distance between A and B is 180km. Draw the distance-time graphs
for these trains on the same axes. When do they pass each other?

Other Graphs 1, 2 & 3 (cont)

5 **The cost of hiring a car is £30 plus an extra charge of 30p per mile.**

a) Complete this table:

Miles	0	10	20	30	50	100
Cost (£)	30	33				

b) On the axes opposite draw a graph to show the cost of hiring the car for up to 100 miles.

c) Use the graph to estimate how much it would cost to hire a car for a 52 mile journey.

....

6 **These sketch graphs show the cost of running a business over several months. Identify which sketch matches each of these descriptions:**

a) Costs are rising steadily. ....

b) Costs are falling after reaching a peak. ....

c) Costs are rising at an increasing rate. ....

d) Costs have been rising but are now levelling out. ....

7 **a)** If £1 = $1.4 complete the table to convert pounds sterling (£) to US dollars ($).

Pounds (£)	10	20	30	40
US Dollars ($)				

b) On the axes opposite draw the graph to convert pounds (£) to US dollars ($).

c) Use your graph to convert $30 into pounds.

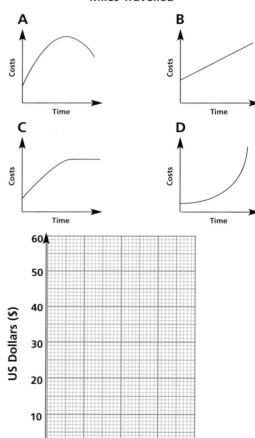

....

8 **Three plumbers A, B and C charge as follows: A – Call out charge £20 then £10 per hour extra.**
B – Call out charge £30 then £5 per hour extra.   C – Standard charge £50 regardless of time.
a) Draw a graph for each plumber's charges on the same axes, for up to 5 hrs work.
b) Which plumber is cheapest for a 30 minute job?
c) Which plumber is cheapest for a $2\frac{1}{2}$ hour job?
d) After what time will plumber C become the cheapest?

Angles 1 & 2

1 **For each diagram work out the size of angle p and angle q, giving a reason for your answer.**

They are not drawn to scale.

a)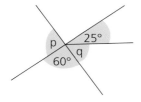

Angle p= ....

Reason: ....

....

Angle q= ....

Reason: ....

....

b)

Angle p= ....

Reason: ....

....

Angle q= ....

Reason: ....

....

c)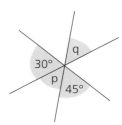

Angle p= ....

Reason: ....

....

Angle q= ....

Reason: ....

....

d)

Angle p= ....

Reason: ....

....

Angle q= ....

Reason: ....

....

e)

Angle p= ....

Reason: ....

....

Angle q= ....

Reason: ....

....

f)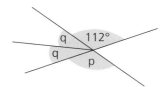

Angle p= ....

Reason: ....

....

Angle q= ....

Reason: ....

....

2 **For each diagram work out the size of angle c and angle d giving a reason for your answer.**

They are not drawn to scale.

a)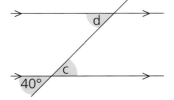

Angle c= ....

Reason: ....

....

Angle d= ....

Reason: ....

....

b)

Angle c= ....

Reason: ....

....

Angle d= ....

Reason: ....

....

c)

Angle c= ....

Reason: ....

....

Angle d= ....

Reason: ....

....

Angles 1 & 2 (cont)

3 For each diagram work out the size of angle m and angle n giving a reason for your answer. They are not drawn to scale.

a)

Angle m=...

Reason: ....

....

Angle n= ....

Reason: ....

....

b)

Angle m=...

Reason: ....

....

Angle n= ....

Reason: ....

....

c)

Angle m=...

Reason: ....

....

Angle n= ....

Reason: ....

....

4 Work out the size of the angles marked a, b and c, giving reasons for your answer. The diagram is not drawn to scale.

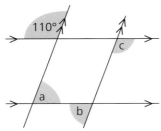

....

....

....

....

5 Work out the size of the angles marked p, q, r and s, giving reasons for your answer. The diagram is not drawn to scale.

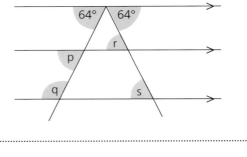

....

....

....

....

6 For each diagram work out the size of x. They are not drawn to scale.

a)   **b)**   **c)**   **d)**

7 For each diagram work out the size of the angles marked giving reasons for your answer. They are not drawn to scale.

a)   **b)**   **c)**

Triangles

1 Draw a diagram and write a short explanation to prove that the interior angles of a triangle add up to 180°.

....

....

....

....

....

2 Draw a diagram and write a short explanation to prove that the exterior angle of a triangle is equal to the sum of the interior angles at the other two vertices.

....

....

....

....

....

3 This diagram has six angles marked a, b, c, d, e and f.

a) Work out the size of angle a in terms of angle b.

b) Work out the size of angle a in terms of angles d and f.

c) Work out the size of angle a in terms of angles c and e.

d) What do angles a, c and e add up to?

The triangle diagram shows angles c and d at the top vertex, b at the lower left vertex with a below it on the extended line, and f and e at the lower right vertex on the extended line.

Types of Triangle

1 Below are four triangles. For each triangle work out the missing angle x and name the type of triangle giving a reason for your answer. They are not drawn to scale.

a)

b)

c)

d)

a)
Angle x =...........................

Type of Triangle:

....

Reason:

....

....

b)
Angle x =...........................

Type of Triangle:

....

Reason:

....

....

c)
Angle x =...........................

Type of Triangle:

....

Reason:

....

....

d)
Angle x =...........................

Type of Triangle:

....

Reason:

....

....

2 For each diagram below work out the size of angle p. They are not drawn to scale.

a)

b)

c)

d)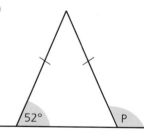

a)
Angle p =.........................

b)
Angle p =...........................

c)
Angle p =...........................

d)
Angle p =...........................

3 The diagram (not drawn to scale) shows a right-angled triangle ABC and an isosceles triangle CDE. Work out the size of the angles marked a and b giving reasons for your answers.

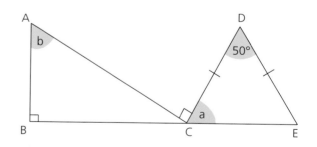

....

....

4 The diagram (not drawn to scale) shows an equilateral triangle ABC and a right-angled triangle CDE. Work out the size of the angles marked m and n giving reasons for your answers.

Quadrilaterals

1 Below are four quadrilaterals. For each quadrilateral work out the missing angle x and name the type of quadrilateral, giving a reason for your answer. They are not drawn to scale.

a)   b)   c)   d)

Angle x = ... Angle x = ... Angle x = ... Angle x = ...

Type of Quadrilateral: Type of Quadrilateral: Type of Quadrilateral: Type of Quadrilateral:

....

Reason: Reason: Reason: Reason:

....

....

2 Which type of quadrilateral am I?

a) I have diagonals that are not equal in length but they bisect each other at right-angles. They also bisect each of my interior angles. ....

b) I have diagonals that are equal in length and bisect each other. However they do not bisect each other at right-angles. ....

c) I have diagonals that are equal in length and bisect each other at right-angles. They also bisect each of my interior angles. ....

3 Draw a diagram and write a short explanation to prove that the interior angles of a quadrilateral add up to 360°.

....
....
....
....
....

4 Calculate the size of the labelled angles in the following diagrams. They are not drawn to scale.

a)   b)   c)   d)

5 **a)** The interior angles of a quadrilateral are $x°$, $2x°$, $3x°$ and $4x°$. Work out the difference in size between the largest angle and the smallest angle in the quadrilateral.

b) The interior angles of a quadrilateral are $x+20°$, $x-30°$, $2x°$ and $110°$. Work out the size of x.

Irregular & Regular Polygons

1 **For each diagram below work out the size of angle p. They are not drawn to scale.**

a)

b)

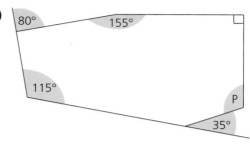

....

....

....

2 **a)** What do the exterior angles of an irregular pentagon add up to?...

   b) What do the exterior angles of a regular pentagon add up to? ....

3 **An irregular polygon has exterior angles equal to 110°, 94°, 88° and 68°.**

   a) How many sides does the polygon have? ....

   b) What is the sum of the interior angles of this irregular polygon?

   ....

   ....

4 **An irregular polygon has interior angles equal to 110°, 155°, 135°, 95°, 140° and 85°.**

   a) How many sides does the polygon have? ....

   b) What is the sum of the exterior angles of this irregular polygon?

   ....

   ....

5 **An irregular pentagon has four exterior angles equal to 47°, 113°, 55° and 71°. What is the size of the fifth exterior angle?**

   ....

6 **a)** How many sides does a polygon have if the sum of its interior angles is twice the sum of its exterior angles? ....

   b) How many sides does a regular polygon have if each interior angle is equal to each exterior angle?

   ....

   c) How many sides does a polygon have if the sum of its interior angles is equal to the sum of its exterior angles? ....

7 **A regular polygon has five sides.**

Calculate the size of **a)** each exterior angle and **b)** each interior angle.

....
....
....
....
....
....

8 **A regular polygon has six sides.**

Calculate the size of **a)** each exterior angle and **b)** each interior angle.

....
....
....
....
....
....

9 **The diagrams below show regular polygons, centre 0. For each polygon work out the size of the angles marked a and b.**

a)

b)

....
....
....
....

....
....
....
....

10 **Jon reckons that it is possible to have a regular polygon where each interior angle is equal to 150° and each exterior angle is equal to 40°. Is he correct? Explain.**

....
....

11 **A polygon has interior angles equal to $x°$, $x+20°$, $2x°$, $2x-10°$ and 50°.**
a) How many sides does this polygon have?
b) Work out the size of x.
c) What is the size of each exterior angle?

12 **A regular polygon has each interior angle equal to $1\frac{1}{2}$ times each exterior angle.**
a) What is the size of each interior angle?
b) What is the size of each exterior angle?
c) How many sides does this regular polygon have?

13 **A regular polygon has each interior angle equal to 170°. How many sides does it have?**

Congruence & Tessellation

1 **Here are four triangles (not drawn to scale).**

A
B
C
D

a) Peter thinks that triangles B and D are congruent. Is he correct? Explain.

....

....

b) Petra thinks that triangles A and C are congruent. Is she correct? Explain.

....

....

2 **a)** These two triangles are congruent.
They are not drawn to scale.

b) These two quadrilaterals are congruent.
They are not drawn to scale.

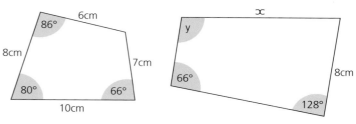

i) What is x? ....

ii) What is y? ....

i) What is x ? ....

ii) What is y? ....

3 **On the isometric grid below draw the tessellation formed using regular hexagons of side 1cm.**

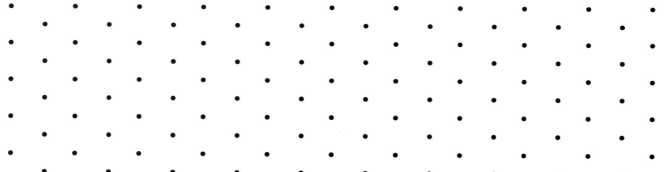

4 Here are three triangles (not drawn to scale).
Which two triangles are congruent? Explain.

5 A regular hexagon will form a tessellation
pattern but a regular pentagon does not.
Explain why.

Similarity

1 **Here are four triangles (not drawn to scale).**

a) Pam thinks that triangles B and C are similar. Is she correct? Explain.

....

....

b) Ian thinks that triangles A and D are similar. Is he correct? Explain.

....

....

2 **These two triangles are similar. Calculate the length of...**

 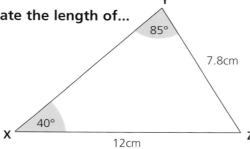

a) XY ....

b) BC ....

3 **In the diagram below BC is parallel to DE. AB = 3 cm, AC = 4cm, BC = 5cm and CE = 2cm.**

The diagram is not drawn to scale.

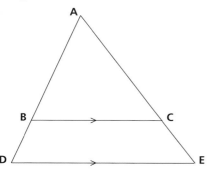

a) Calculate the length of DE.

....

....

....

b) Calculate the length of BD.

....

....

....

4 **Here are three triangles (not drawn to scale).**
Which two triangles are similar? Explain.

Transformations 1

1 **The grid shows twelve shapes A to L.**

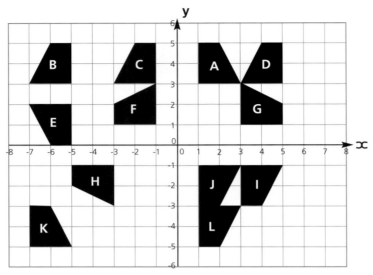

a) Give the letter of the image which is object A reflected...

i) in the x-axis .... **ii)** in the y-axis............................... **iii)** in the line $x = 3$...............................

iv) in the line y = 1............................... **v)** in the line y = x............................... **vi)** in the line y = -x...............................

b) Describe the single reflection which takes B to E. ....

c) Describe the single reflection which takes F to G. ....

2 **Triangles A, B, C and D are all different reflections of the blue triangle. For each one draw in the mirror line and describe the reflection fully.**

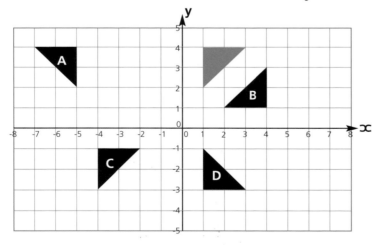

Triangle A: ....

....

Triangle B: ....

....

Triangle C: ....

....

Triangle D: ....

....

3 **A is a triangle with coordinates (3,1), (5,1) and (5,2).**
a) On a suitable grid draw triangle A.
b)i) Reflect triangle A in the line $x = 1$. Label this triangle B. **ii)** Reflect triangle A in the line y = -1. Label this triangle C.
iii) Reflect triangle A in the line y = x. Label this triangle D. **iv)** Reflect triangle A in the line y = -x. Label this triangle E.

1 **The grid shows ten shapes A to J.**

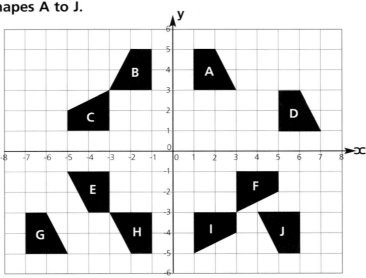

a) Give the letter of the image which is object A rotated...

i) ¼ turn clockwise about the origin (0,0) ....

ii) ½ turn clockwise about the origin (0,0) ....

iii) ¾ turn clockwise about the origin (0,0) ....

b) Describe the single rotation which takes C to A. ....

2 **The grid shows triangle A.**

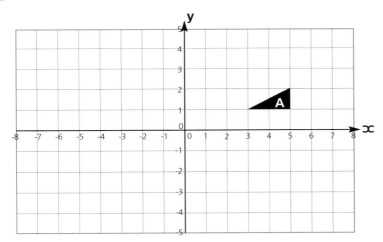

a) Rotate triangle A ¼ turn clockwise about the origin (0,0). Label this triangle B.

b) Rotate triangle A ½ turn clockwise about the origin (0,0). Label this triangle C.

c) Rotate triangle A ¾ turn clockwise about the origin (0,0). Label this triangle D.

3 **A is a quadrilateral with coordinates (2,2), (4,4), (5,3) and (5,1).**

a) On a suitable grid draw quadrilateral A.

b) i) Rotate quadrilateral A ¼ turn clockwise about the origin (0,0). Label this quadrilateral B. **ii)** Rotate quadrilateral A ½ turn clockwise about the origin (0,0). Label this quadrilateral C. **iii)** Rotate quadrilateral A ¾ turn clockwise about the origin (0,0). Label this quadrilateral D.

Transformations 3

1 **The grid shows ten shapes A to J.**

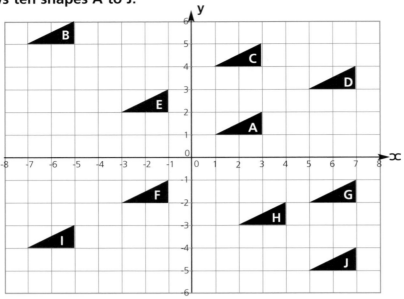

a) Give the letter of the shape which is shape A translated by the vector...

i) $\begin{pmatrix} 4 \\ 2 \end{pmatrix}$ ....

ii) $\begin{pmatrix} 1 \\ -4 \end{pmatrix}$ ....

iii) $\begin{pmatrix} -4 \\ 1 \end{pmatrix}$ ....

iv) $\begin{pmatrix} 0 \\ 3 \end{pmatrix}$ ....

v) $\begin{pmatrix} -8 \\ -5 \end{pmatrix}$ ....

vi) $\begin{pmatrix} 4 \\ -6 \end{pmatrix}$ ....

b) What is the translation vector which maps triangle D onto triangle A? ....

c) What is the translation vector which maps triangle B onto triangle A? ....

2 **The grid shows triangle A. Draw and label the following translations.**

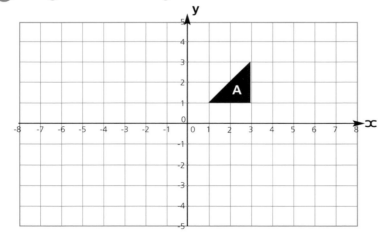

a) Triangle A is mapped onto triangle B by the translation vector $\begin{pmatrix} 4 \\ 2 \end{pmatrix}$

b) Triangle A is mapped onto triangle C by the translation vector $\begin{pmatrix} -5 \\ -4 \end{pmatrix}$

c) Triangle A is mapped onto triangle D by the translation vector $\begin{pmatrix} -8 \\ 0 \end{pmatrix}$

d) Triangle A is mapped onto triangle E by the translation vector $\begin{pmatrix} 5 \\ -6 \end{pmatrix}$

3 **A is a triangle with coordinates (-1,-3), (-3,-2) and (-4,4).**
   a) On a suitable grid draw triangle A.
   b)i) Translate triangle A by the vector $\begin{pmatrix} 5 \\ 5 \end{pmatrix}$ Label this triangle B. **ii)** Translate triangle A by the vector $\begin{pmatrix} -5 \\ -5 \end{pmatrix}$ Label this triangle C.

   iii) Translate triangle A by the vector $\begin{pmatrix} 5 \\ -5 \end{pmatrix}$ Label this triangle D. **iv)** Translate triangle A by the vector $\begin{pmatrix} -5 \\ 5 \end{pmatrix}$ Label this triangle E.

1 The grid shows triangle A.

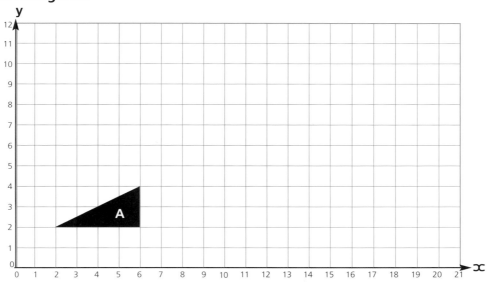

Enlarge triangle A by...

a) a scale factor of 3 about the centre of enlargement (0,0). Label this triangle B.

b) a scale factor of 2 about the centre of enlargement (0,3). Label this triangle C.

c) a scale factor of 2 about the centre of enlargement (4,0). Label this triangle E.

2 The grid shows two quadrilaterals A and B.

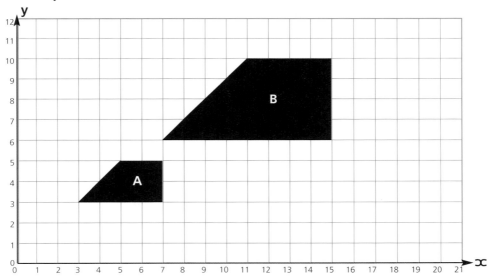

Describe fully the enlargement that would map quadrilateral A onto B.

....

....

3 **Triangle A has coordinates (3,2), (6,2) and (6,4). a)** On a suitable grid draw triangle A.
b) Complete the following enlargements: **i)** Triangle A is enlarged by a scale factor of 2, centre of enlargement (0,0).
Label this triangle B. **ii)** Triangle A is enlarged by a scale factor of ½, centre of enlargement (0,0). Label this triangle C.
iii) Triangle A is enlarged by a scale factor of 3, centre of enlargement (1,1). Label this triangle D.

Coordinates 1

1 Write down the coordinates of the

letters A to H on the graph opposite.

A ....
E ....

B ....
F ....

C ....
G ....

D ....
H ....

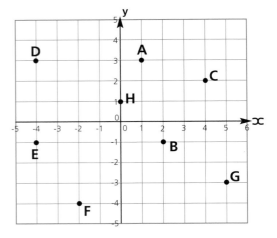

2 Write down the coordinates of each of the

vertices (corners) of this box.

A ....
E ....

B ....
F ....

C ....
G ....

D ....

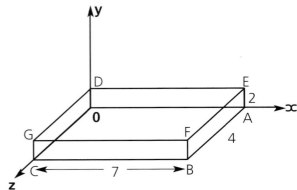

3 This cube has a side length of 5cm.

a) Write down the coordinates of each of the vertices.

A ....
E ....

B ....
F ....

C ....
G ....

D ....

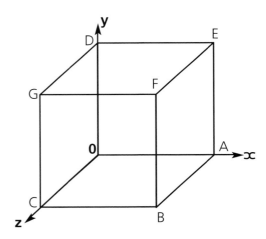

b) What are the coordinates of the point of intersection of the two

diagonals OB and AC?

....

c) What are the coordinates of the point of intersection of the two diagonals OF and AG?

....

4 Draw axes from -5 to 5 on the x-axis and -3 to 4 on the y-axis.
a) Draw and label A (4,2), B (-5,2), C (-4,2)
b) Draw and label a fourth coordinate D to produce a parallelogram ABCD.

5 A cube has a side length of 3cm. Its four base coordinates are at (0,0,0), (3,0,0), (3,3,0) and (0,3,0).
Draw a 3D graph and write down the other 4 coordinates.

Coordinates 2

1 a) On the graph opposite, plot the coordinates
A(1,2), B(3,5), C(7,6) and D(7,3).

b) Find the coordinates of the midpoint, M,
of the line segments:

i) AB ....

....

ii) BC ....

....

iii) CD ....

....

iv) AD ....

....

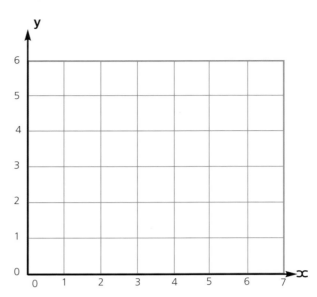

2 a) On the graph opposite, plot the coordinates
P(3,1), Q(0,3), R(4,6), S(7,4).

b) Find the coordinates of the midpoint , M,
of the line segments:

i) PQ ....

....

....

....

....

ii) QR ....

....

....

....

....

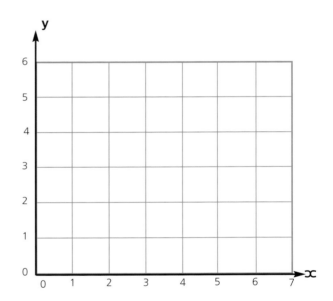

iii) RS ....   **iv)** SP ....

....

....

....

....

---

3 The line segment XY has coordinates (-2,-1) and (6,4) respectively. Find the coordinates of the midpoint M.

4 Hexagon ABCDEF has coordinates A(-2,3), B(2,3), C(4,0), D(2,-4), E (-2,-4), F(-4,0).
   a) Plot these on a graph to produce a hexagon.
   b) Find the coordinates of the midpoint, M, for line segments: **i)** AF **ii)** BC **iii)** CD **iv)** EF.

Perimeter 1 & 2

1 **Calculate the perimeter of the following shapes...**

a)

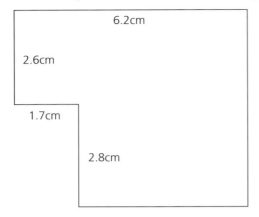

6.2cm

2.6cm

1.7cm

2.8cm

....

....

b)

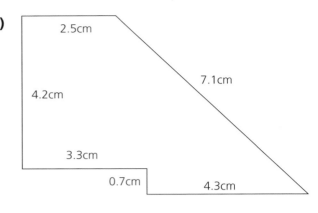

2.5cm

7.1cm

4.2cm

3.3cm

0.7cm

4.3cm

....

....

c)

....

....

d)

....

....

e)

....

....

f)

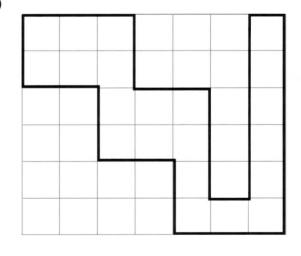

....

....

Perimeter 1 & 2 (cont)

2 Calculate the circumference of the following circles to 1 decimal place, centre 0. Take π = 3.14.

a)

b)

c)

d)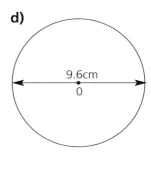

....
....
....
....

3 A window is in the shape of a semi-circle on top of a rectangle as shown in the diagram.
If AB = 1.8m and BC = 90cm, calculate the perimeter of the window to 1 decimal place.
Take π = 3.14.

D ---------- C

A ————— B

....
....
....
....
....
....
....

4 Mrs Jones' garden is rectangular. At each end there is a semi-circular flower bed and the rest
of the garden is lawn, as shown in the diagram. If AB = 10m and BC = 8m, calculate the
perimeter of the lawn. Take π = 3.14.

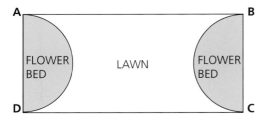

....
....
....
....

---

5 A window measures 200cm by 100cm. Calculate the perimeter of the window.

6 A wall measures 3.6m by 15m Calculate the perimeter of the wall.

7 Calculate the circumference of the following circles to 1 decimal place. Take π = 3.14.
a) Radius = 12cm **b)** Radius = 1.2cm **c)** Diameter = 12cm **d)** Diameter = 120cm

Area 1, 2 & 3

1 Calculate an approximate area for the following shapes. Each square has an area of 1cm².

a)

b)

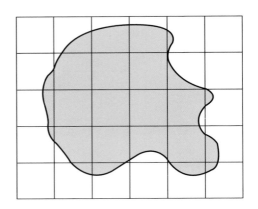

....

2 Calculate the area of the following shapes. They are not drawn to scale. Take π = 3.14.

a)

b)

c)

....
....

d)

e)

f)

....
....

g)

h)

i)

....
....

3 A circular table has a radius of 0.8m.
Calculate its area to 1 d.p. Take π = 3.14.

....

....

....

4 A circular flower bed has a diameter of 4.6m.
Calculate its area to 1 d.p. Take π = 3.14.

....

....

....

5 Calculate the area of the following shapes to 1 d.p. They are not drawn to scale. Take π = 3.14.

a)

b)

....

....

....

....

....

6 Calculate the surface area of the following solids to 1 d.p.

a)

b)

....

....

....

....

7 A property developer decides to varnish the floorboards in the living room of one of his houses. A plan of the floor is shown alongside.
It is not to scale. One tin of varnish will cover 16m² and costs £4.99.
If he wants to apply two coats of varnish to the whole floor, how much will it cost him?

8 Deduce the formula for the area of a) a parallelogram b) a triangle.

Volume

1 Calculate the volume of the following solids:

a)

b)

c)

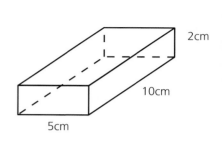

....
....
....
....

2 Calculate the volume of the following solids:

a)

b) to 3 sig. fig.

c) to 3 sig. fig.

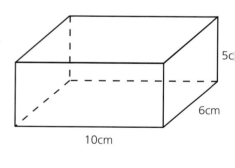

....
....
....
....

3 The following solids all have a volume of 100cm³. For each solid calculate the missing length represented by x.

a)   b)

4 A cuboid has length 200cm, width 160cm and height 150cm. Calculate a) its volume in cm³ b) its volume in m³.

3-D Shapes 1 & 2

1 **a)** What shape is the base of the

cuboid shown opposite? ....

b) Which edges are equal in

length to CD?...

c) Which lengths are equal to AH?..

d) How many vertices has the cuboid? ....

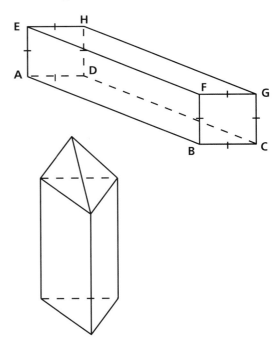

2 **An equilateral triangular prism has a tetrahedron**

placed on top of it. For this combined solid...

a) How many edges does it have? ....

b) How many vertices? ....

c) How many faces? ....

3 **On the grid below draw full size diagrams of the following solids.**

a)

2cm 2cm
3cm

b)

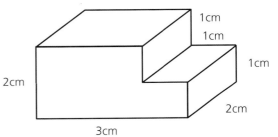

1cm
1cm
1cm
2cm
2cm
3cm

4 **Draw a sketch of the plan view of this**

square-based pyramid.

3-D Shapes 1 & 2 (cont)

⑤ The diagram alongside shows a solid. Draw and label an accurate diagram of the solid showing...

a) plan view   **b)** front elevation   **c)** side elevation

⑥ A net of a solid is shown opposite.

a) What is the name of the 3-D solid?

....

b) How many vertices does it have?

....

c) Which other corners meet at D? Put an X on each one.

d) How many planes of symmetry does the solid have?

....

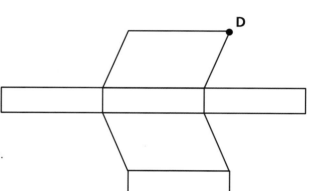

⑦ Which of the following are nets for a triangular prism? Place a tick beside the correct net(s).

a)

b)

c)

d)

⑧ Draw an accurate full-size net of a regular hexagonal prism if each edge is 3cm long.

⑨ How many planes of symmetry does a cube have?

⑩ Draw the **a)** plan **b)** front elevation **c)** side elevation of this solid.

1 **Draw all the lines of symmetry for each of the following shapes:**

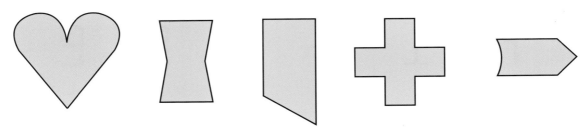

2 **Mark on the lines of symmetry for each of these letters:**

M S H B Z A V C K

3 **How many lines of symmetry do each of the following quadrilaterals have?**

a) square .... ☐

b) Rectangle .... ▭

c) Parallelogram .... ▱

d) Rhombus .... ◊

e) Kite .... ◁

f) Trapezium .... ◁

4 **For each of the following shapes draw in all the lines of symmetry and write down the order of rotational symmetry.**

a)

b)

c)

Order of rotational symmetry:

....

Order of rotational symmetry:

....

Order of rotational symmetry:

....

5 **What is the order of rotational symmetry for each of these letters?**

X   H   I   Z   K   S   E   N

....

6 **What is the order of rotational symmetry for each of these shapes?**

a)   b)   c)   d)

   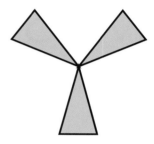

Order:........................   Order:........................   Order:........................   Order:........................

7 **a)** Draw accurately a regular pentagon with sides 3cm long and internal angles 108°.

b) Mark on the lines of symmetry.

c) What is the order of rotational symmetry?

....

8 **a)** Draw a regular hexagon. Interior angles are 120°.
b) Draw in all lines of symmetry and write down the order of rotational symmetry.

9 **Write down the order of rotational symmetry for each quadrilateral:**
a) Square **b)** Rectangle **c)** Parallelogram **d)** Rhombus **e)** Kite **f)** Trapezium.

Scale Drawings and Map Scales

1 a) Draw an accurate scale drawing of this garden, using a scale of 1cm to represent 2.5m.

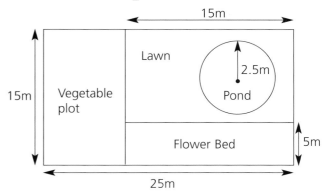

b) What is the actual diagonal distance across the garden from corner to corner in metres?

....

2 This is part of a map of Devon and Cornwall drawn to a scale of 1cm : 10km.

a) What is the direct distance from Launceston to Exeter?

....

....

b) What is the direct distance between Bodmin and Looe?

....

....

c) Which two places are a direct distance of 43km from Tavistock

....

....

3 Draw an accurate scale drawing of a rectangular field 80m long and 50m wide. By measurement, find the actual distance diagonally from one corner to the opposite corner, to the nearest metre.

4 The diagram alongside shows a sketch of one side of a house.
  a) Draw an accurate scale drawing using a scale of 1cm to 1m.
  b) By measurement, find the actual height of the house (x).

Measuring Bearings

1 The diagram shows the position of the coastguard (C), the beach (B) and a yacht (Y).

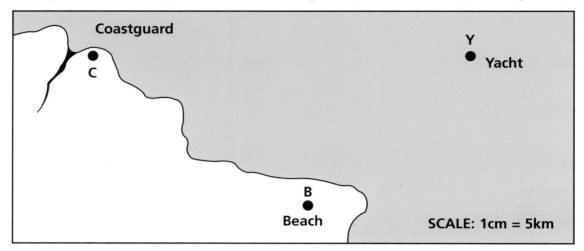

a) What is the bearing of...

i) Y from C? .... **ii)** Y from B? ....

iii) B from C? .... **iv)** B from Y? ....

v) C from Y? .... **vi)** C from B? ....

b) What is the actual distance from...

i) C to B? .... **ii)** C to Y? .... **iii)** B to Y? ....

2 The map shows the position of 4 towns A, B, C and D on an island.

A helicopter flies directly from A to B, then B to C, then C to D and finally D back to A.

On what four bearings must it fly?

A ➤ B ....

B ➤ C ....

C ➤ D ....

D ➤ A ....

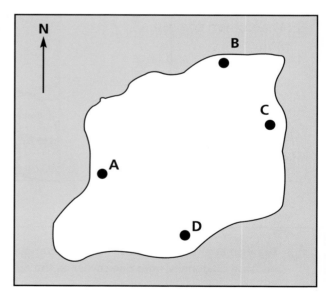

3 An explorer walks 1 000m on a bearing of 070° and then walks 2 000m on a bearing of 160°.
 a) Draw an accurate scale drawing of his route.
 b) By measurement, find the bearing he must follow to return directly to his starting point.

4 Treasure is buried on an island according to the following instructions: "The treasure lies on a bearing of 100° from the coconut tree and on a bearing of 200° from the cactus plant. The cactus plant is 20m due east of the coconut tree." Draw a scale drawing using 1cm to 5m to show the position of the treasure.

Reading Scales

1 **a)** Write down the readings on the following thermometers.

i)

....

ii)

....

iii)

....

b) Write down the readings on the following weighing scales.

i) .... ii) .... iii) ....

2 Write down the number of minutes and seconds which have elapsed on these stopwatches. Minutes are shown on the smaller dial.

a) .... b) .... c) ....

---

3 Draw a diagram of a clinical thermometer with a scale from 30° to 40° measured in 0.5 degree intervals.
Show **a)** 37.5°C **b)** 32.0°C **c)** 35.5°C **d)** 39.25°C

4 Draw a diagram of a weighing scale which weighs a maximum of 3.6kg and has 100g intervals.

Converting Measurements

1 **Convert...**

a) 450cm into metres

b) 3.5 litres into millilitres

c) 1.25kg into grams

d) 6 874g into kg

e) 45km into metres

f) 0.55cm into mm

2 **Convert these lengths into metres.**

a) 1 005cm

b) 1.937km

c) 2 650mm

3 **Put these weights into order of size, smallest first.**

420g, 4kg, 39.5kg, 4 220mg, 0.405kg

4 **Convert...**

a) 45cm into inches

b) 6 ounces into grams

c) 5 gallons into litres

5 **Terry is 1.5m tall. Jake is 68 inches tall. Who is the tallest and by how much?**

6 **Put these lengths into decreasing order of size:**
1km, 900m, 1 200m, 11 000cm, 1 050 000mm

7 **Convert...**
a) 3 miles into km **b)** 12km into miles **c)** 4.5 pounds into grams **d)** 360g into pounds **e)** 12 pints into litres
f) 22.5 litres into pints

8 **Sue ran a 10km race. How many yards did she run altogether? (1760 yards = 1 mile).**

1 A sprinter covers 100m in 10.0s. Calculate his speed in m/s.

2 A long jumper covers 8 metres in 0.5 seconds. Calculate his speed in m/s.

3 How long does it take a car to travel 280km at an average speedof 80km/h?

4 Work out the time taken to travel 92km at an average speed of 55km/h.

5 A marathon runner completes 26.2 miles in a course record of 2hrs 20mins. What was his average speed?

6 A tortoise takes 20 minutes to get from one end of the garden to the other. His average speed was 2cm per second. How long is the garden in metres?

7 A boat travels for $2\frac{1}{2}$ hours at 100km/h and then $1\frac{1}{2}$ hours at 80km/h. Calculate its average speed for the whole journey.

8 A cyclist covers 1000m in 1 minute. Calculate his speed in km/h.

9 A car travels 30 metres per second for $3\frac{1}{2}$ hours. How far does it travel in km?

Constructions 1 & 2

1 Construct a triangle ABC with sides AB 4cm, BC 3cm and angle ABC = 40°.

2 Construct a triangle PQR where PQ is 6cm, QR is 5cm and PR is 2cm.

3 The sketch opposite shows three towns A, B and C.
B is on a bearing of 040° from A. C is due East of
A and B is on a bearing of 300° from C. C is 40km
from A. Construct an accurate scale drawing of this
diagram in the space below.

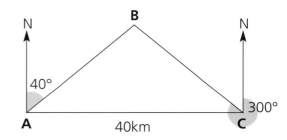

4 Use a pair of compasses and a ruler to construct a regular hexagon inside a circle.

Properties of Circles

1 Name each of the parts of the circle labelled A to F opposite.

a) A ....

b) B ....

c) C ....

d) D ....

e) E ....

f) F ....

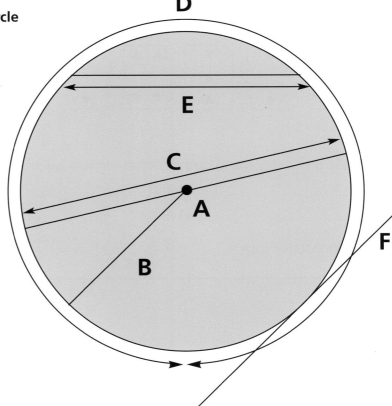

2 In the space below draw a circle with a radius of 4.5cm. Draw a tangent at the point where the radius touches the circumference, and then draw a chord which measures 7cm.

3 Write a brief definition for the following: **a)** Circumference **b)** Radius **c)** Diameter **d)** Chord **e)** Tangent **f)** Arc

Probability...

1 **Tim has ten cards (shown below). They are placed face down and mixed up.**

a) What is the probability that a card picked at random will be...

i) a 2? .... **ii)** a 3? .... **iii)** a 4? ....

iv) a 5? .... **v)** not a 2? .... **vi)** not a 3? ....

b) Here is a probability scale:

On the scale above ....

i) mark with an A the probability that a card picked at random will be a 2.

ii) mark with a B the probability that a card picked at random will be a 3.

iii) mark with a C the probability that a card picked at random will be a 4.

iv) mark with a D the probability that a card picked at random will be a 5.

2 **A bag contains 4 red counters, 5 blue counters and 9 yellow counters.**

A counter is picked out at random. What is the probability that it is ...

a) red? .... **b)** not red? .... **c)** blue? ....

d) not blue? .... **e)** yellow? .... **f)** not yellow? ....

3 **A page in a calendar shows the following month of June.**

If a date is chosen at random, what is the probability that it is...

a) an even number? .... **b)** an odd number? ....

c) a prime number? .... **d)** a weekday? ....

e) not a weekday? ....

4 **Jack has the following spinner. He spins it.**

a) What is the probability that the spinner does not land on a 1?

....

b) What is the probability that the spinner does not land on a 2?

....

c) What is the probability that the spinner lands on a 3?

....

...Mutually Exclusive Outcomes

5 Vicky has two sets of cards, A and B as shown below:

a) Complete all the possible outcomes if two cards are picked, one from A and one from B, at random.

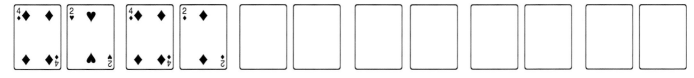

b) What is the probability that the two cards picked are **i)** both 2s? ....

ii) both the same suit? .... **iii)** not the same suit?....................................

6 Brian's pencil case contains blue, black, red and green biros only. The probability of picking out a biro of a certain colour is shown in the table. What is the probability that the biro picked out is red?

Colour of biro	Probability of picking that colour
Blue	0.2
Black	0.35
Red	....
Green	0.15

7 On her way to work, Safia has to drive through a set of traffic lights. The probability that Safia will arrive at work on time is 0.4 and that she will arrive late is 0.25. What is the probability that she will arrive early?

....

8 A bag contains 8 blue marbles, 6 red marbles and 2 green marbles. One marble is pulled out at random and not replaced back into the bag. A second marble is then picked out at random.

a) What is the probability that the second marble picked out is blue, if the first marble picked out was green? ....

b) What is the probability that the second marble picked out is green, if the first marble picked out was also green? ....

---

9 A box contains 7 red balls and 3 blue balls. A ball is picked out at random.
What is the probability that it is **a)** red? **b)** not red? **c)** blue? **d)** not blue? **e)** red or blue? **f)** black?

10 A kitchen cupboard contains tins of baked beans, peas, carrots and potatoes only. The probability of picking a tin of potatoes is $\frac{1}{12}$, while the probability of picking a tin of carrots is three times that of a tin of potatoes, and a tin of peas is twice that of a tin of carrots.
a) What is the probability of picking **i)** a tin of carrots? **ii)** a tin of peas? **iii)** a tin of baked beans?
b) What is the probability of not picking **i)** a tin of carrots? **ii)** a tin of peas? **iii)** a tin of baked beans?
c) If the cupboard contains 4 tins of baked beans, how many tins are there in the cupboard altogether?

Listing All Outcomes

1 **Two dice are thrown. The two numbers are added together to give a total score.**

a) Complete the sample space diagram below to show all the scores:

	First Die					
	1	2	3	4	5	6
Second Die 1	2	3	4			
2	3	4				
3	4					
4						
5						
6						

b) What is the probability that the total score will be ...

i) equal to 7? ....

ii) greater than 7? ....

iii) a prime number? ....

iv) a square number? ....

v) greater than 12? ....

vi) a multiple of 3? ....

vii) a factor of 12? ....

2 **Francis has the following coins in her pocket:**

Jim has the following coins in his pocket:

Two coins are picked out at random, one from Francis' pocket and one from Jim's pocket.

The values of the two coins are added together to give a total.

a) Complete the sample space diagram below to show all the values:

	Francis' Coin					
Jim's Coin						

b) What is the probability that the total value of the two coins added together is ...

i) equal to 6p? ....

ii) equal to 11p? ....

iii) less than 10p? ....

iv) greater than 40p? ....

v) less than 40p? ....

vi) equal to 40p? ....

---

3 **Bruce has an ordinary die. Robin has the following spinner:**
The spinner is spun and the dice is thrown to give two numbers.

a) Draw a sample space diagram to show all the possible scores if the numbers are multiplied together.

b) What is the probability that the score is **i)** equal to 12? **ii)** equal to 24? **iii)** a multiple of 10?
iv) a factor of 4? **v)** an odd number? **vi)** an even number?

Estimated Probability

1 **The following spinner is spun 120 times:**

a) How many times would you expect the spinner to land on ...

i) a 1? .... **ii)** a 2? .... **iii)** a 3? ....

b) The actual number of times the spinner landed on a 1, 2 and 3 is shown in the table below. For each number calculate the estimated probability.

Number	Number of times landed	Estimated probability
1	66	....
2	38	....
3	16	....

2 **Jane tosses a coin 50, 100, 150, 200 and 250 times. She records the number of tails she gets in a table (shown alongside):**

a) Complete the table by calculating the missing estimated probability.

b) On the grid below draw a bar graph to show the estimated probability of the coin landing on tails.

Number of tosses	Number of tails	Estimated probability
50	20	0.4
100	44	....
150	80	....
200	92	....
250	120	....

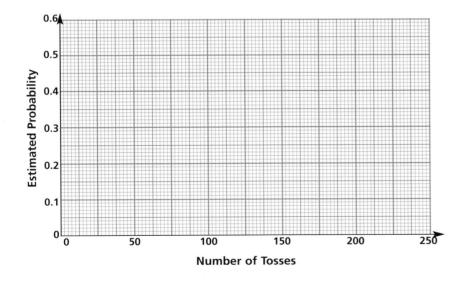

c) If Jane kept tossing the coin, what would you expect the estimated probability of the coin landing on tails to become? Explain why.

....

....

....

....

....

....

3 **Below are the results of an experiment where a die was thrown and the number of 6s were recorded.**

Number of throws	30	60	90	120	150	180	210	240	270	300	330	360
Number of 6s thrown	3	5	10	16	23	28	35	42	47	49	52	59
Estimated probability												

a) Complete the table by calculating the missing estimated probability.

b) Draw a bar graph to show the estimated probability of throwing a 6.

c) How many 6s would you expect to be thrown if the experiment was continued and the die was thrown 1500 times?

Collecting Data 1 & 2

1 **What is the difference between primary data and secondary data?**

....

....

....

2 **a)** What is sampling?

....

....

b) A recent survey carried out in Manchester suggests that 90% of the national population prefer football to rugby. The survey was conducted on 200 males. Has this survey provided reliable data? Explain why.

....

....

....

....

....

3 **Jenny is concerned about the breakfast habits of the pupils in her school. She decides to use a questionnaire to find out what pupils have to eat for breakfast. She has chosen eight questions for her questionnaire. Decide whether each question is suitable or not suitable, giving a reason for your answer.**

a) Everybody should eat breakfast. Don't you agree?

....

b) Do you eat breakfast?

....

c) What time do you get up in the morning?

....

d) Are you a vegetarian?

....

e) What year are you?

....

f) What do you have to eat if you have breakfast?

....

g) If you eat breakfast do you have cereal, toast or other?

....

h) Do you brush your teeth before breakfast?

....

4 Joe works in a supermarket. He decides to use a questionnaire to find out about the shopping habits of the customers who come into the store. Here is the first question:

'How old are you?' Tick the correct box

Under 10 years		11 years to 20 years		21 years to 40 years		41 years to 60 years		61 years to 80 years		Over 80 years	

a) Make up two more suitable questions Joe could use for his questionnaire.

....

....

b) Make up two questions which would not be suitable for his questionnaire.

....

....

5 In a survey a group of pupils were asked, 'How long did you spend watching TV over the weekend?'

a) Design a suitable observation sheet to collect this information.

b) How would you make sure that the information obtained was from a random sample?

....

....

6 Molly works in a pizza parlour. She decides to use a questionnaire to find out about the eating habits of the people who come into the parlour.
  a) Make up three suitable questions Molly could use for her questionnaire.
  b) Make up three questions which are not suitable for her questionnaire.

7 Jimmy is carrying out a survey to investigate what the pupils in his school spend their pocket money on.
  a) Design a suitable observation sheet for him to collect the information.
  b) How could Jimmy make sure that the information collected was random?

Sorting Data 1 & 2

1 **What is the difference between discrete and continuous data?**

....

....

....

....

2 **Jane is carrying out a traffic survey. She records the number of cars that pass her house every 30 seconds for a period of 20 minutes. Group her data by completing the frequency table below.**

Number of cars

4	3	4	✗	2	5	5	4	3	2
4	5	3	2	4	4	4	5	5	✗
2	4	3	5	4	3	3	5	2	4
2	4	3	5	2	✗	✗	4	5	3

Number of cars	Tally	Frequency
1	IIII	4
2		
3		
4		
5		

3 **A survey was carried out on the number of residents in each house on a street.**

The results are given below:

4 , 5 , 3 , 4 , 3 , 6 , 1 , 5 , 4 , 2 , 3 , 4 , 5 , 2 , 4 , 5 , 5 , 3 , 4 , 6
4, 2 , 5 , 3 , 5 , 2 , 4 , 3 , 4 , 1 , 3 , 4 , 4 , 1 , 5 , 2 , 4 , 5 , 3 , 4

a) In the space below group together the results in a frequency table.

b) What percentage of the houses have 3 or more residents? ....

4 The test results for a group of students are given below.

Group the data to complete the frequency table below.

31	61	40	63	65
78	52	57	~~15~~	35
77	~~11~~	68	46	68
64	70	26	87	49

Test Mark	Tally	Frequency
0-19	II	2
20-39		
40-59		
60-79		
80-99		

5 John has recorded the temperature at midday every day for the month of June using a thermometer. All the temperatures are to the nearest degree Celsius.

a) Group together John's results by completing the frequency table.

JUNE

		1 7°C	2 11°C	3 11°C	4 13°C	5 16°C
6 17°C	7 16°C	8 15°C	9 13°C	10 13°C	11 16°C	12 14°C
13 8°C	14 9°C	15 15°C	16 14°C	17 14°C	18 18°C	19 17°C
20 16°C	21 16°C	22 11°C	23 12°C	24 14°C	25 13°C	26 17°C
27 20°C	28 22°C	29 19°C	30 21°C			

Temperature (°C)	Tally	Frequency
$5 \leqslant T < 10$		
$10 \leqslant T < 15$		
$15 \leqslant T < 20$		
$20 \leqslant T < 25$		

b) What percentage of the recorded midday temperatures in June are 15°C or more?

....

6 Bolton Wanderers scored the following number of goals in Premier League matches for the 2002/2003 season.
1, 1, 1, 1, 2, 1, 1, 0, 1, 1, 1, 1, 4, 1, 0, 1, 0, 1, 4
0, 0, 0, 1, 0, 1, 4, 1, 1, 0, 2, 1, 2, 0, 1, 0, 2, 0, 2
Group together the data in a frequency table.

7 Emma decided to measure the height (h) of all the students in her class.
Here are the results, to the nearest cm:
171, 178, 166, 173, 180, 173, 186, 176, 170, 184, 178, 174, 169, 189, 175, 182, 181, 171, 179, 164, 178, 175, 174, 191, 169, 178, 173, 188, 167, 192.

a) Sort the data into a frequency table using class intervals $160 \leqslant h < 165$, $165 \leqslant h < 170$ etc.
b) What percentage of the students in Emma's class have a height measurement of 170cm or more?

8 The individual weights of 40 people, to the nearest kg, are as follows:
79, 75, 68, 70, 83, 72, 81, 89, 61, 74, 80, 51, 84, 63, 73, 54, 76, 74, 80, 85, 94, 77, 71, 81, 70, 66, 87, 62, 59, 63, 63, 67, 75, 81, 80, 78, 60, 77, 61, 75.
Sort the data into a frequency table using appropriate class intervals.

Sorting Data 3

1 The following data shows the age (in years) of 30 shoppers in a supermarket.

41 , 51 , 8 , 60 , 21 , 31 , 41 , 17 , 68 , 28 , 34 , 45 , 46 , 52 , 74 , 56 , 10 , 23 , 47 , 30 , 34 , 9 , 42 , 29 , 55 , 44 , 38 , 57 , 47 , 58

Using tens to form the 'stem' and units to form the 'leaves', draw a stem and leaf diagram to show the data.

2 A survey of 120 people was conducted to find out if they listened to the radio whilst driving. Complete the two way table to show the results.

	Men	Women	Total
Listen to radio	32	....	73
Do not listen to radio	....	24	....
Total	55	....	....

3 A survey of 200 Year 7, 8 and 9 pupils was carried out to find their favourite type of music from a choice of three: Pop, Rap or Dance.

a) Complete the two way table to show the results.

	Year 7	Year 8	Year 9	Total
Pop	42	....	18	....
Rap	....	12	....	41
Dance	14	....	31	69
Total	....	....	62	....

b) What percentage of the pupils chose Pop as their favourite type of music?

....

4 Here are the heights, to the nearest cm, of 30 students in a class:
171, 178, 166, 173, 180, 173, 186, 176, 170, 184, 178, 174, 169, 189, 175, 182, 181, 171, 179, 164, 178, 175, 174, 191, 169, 178, 173, 188, 167, 192.
a) Using tens to form the 'stem' and units to form the 'leaves' draw a stem and leaf digram to show the data.
b) What is the modal class of the data?
c) What is the median value of the data?

78 | **HANDLING DATA** | Revision Guide Reference: Page 85 | *Lonsdale* REVISION GUIDES

Displaying Data 1

1 A survey was carried out to find the favourite type of music for a group of people. The results are displayed in this pictogram.

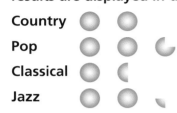

Country ⬤ ⬤
Pop ⬤ ⬤ ◖
Classical ⬤ ◖
Jazz ⬤ ⬤ ◣
Rock ⬤ ◣

Where ⬤ represents four people.

Draw a bar graph to show this information.

2 36 primary school children were asked to name their favourite pet.

$\frac{1}{3}$ said DOG

$\frac{1}{4}$ said CAT

$\frac{2}{9}$ said FISH

$\frac{1}{12}$ said RABBIT

... and the remainder said BIRD.

Draw a bar graph to show this information.

3 This bar chart shows the different types of milk sold in a supermarket and the actual number of pints sold, on one day.

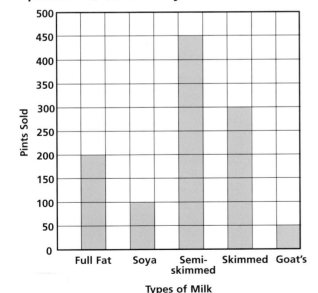

a) What was the second most popular type of milk sold?

....

b) How many pints of milk are sold in total?

....

c) In the space below draw a pictogram to show this data:

4 Draw **a)** a pictogram and **b)** a bar graph to show the data recorded in question **2** on page 78.

5 Repeat for question **3** on page 78.

Displaying Data 2

1 The table shows the height of a girl from birth to age 5. Her height was recorded every year on her birthday.

Height (cm)	42	51	66	75	84	89
Time (years)	0	1	2	3	4	5

Draw a time series to show the trend in her height.

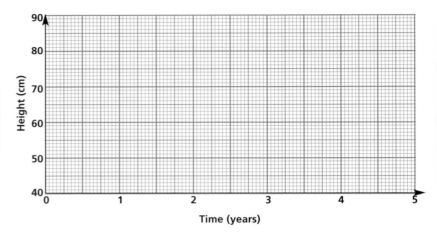

2 In a survey 50 women were asked how much they spend on cosmetics in one week. The results are shown in the table below.

Money Spent, M (£)	Frequency
$0 \leqslant M < 2$	1
$2 \leqslant M < 4$	6
$4 \leqslant M < 6$	28
$6 \leqslant M < 8$	11
$8 \leqslant M < 10$	4

a) Draw a frequency polygon to show the information.

b) 50 men were also asked how much they spend on cosmetics in one week. The results are shown below. On the same axes draw a frequency polygon to show the money spent by men.

Money Spent, M (£)	Frequency
$0 \leqslant M < 2$	13
$2 \leqslant M < 4$	28
$4 \leqslant M < 6$	5
$6 \leqslant M < 8$	3
$8 \leqslant M < 10$	1

c) How do the two distributions compare?

....

....

....

....

....

....

....

....

3 Below are the highest recorded temperatures, in °C, on one particular day for forty places around the world.

17, 28, 33, 19, 21, 28, 31, 24, 21, 20, 19, 28, 24, 19, 20, 24, 29, 32, 16, 26,

33, 24, 23, 16, 16, 20, 28, 17, 24, 23, 26, 31, 33, 18, 31, 26, 28, 19, 19, 21

a) Group together the data in a frequency table.

b) Construct a frequency diagram to show the data.

c) On separate axes construct a frequency polygon to show the data.

Scatter Diagrams 1 & 2

1 This scatter diagram shows the average journey time and distance travelled for ten pupils travelling from home to school.

a) What does the scatter diagram tell you about the relationship between the journey time and the distance travelled?

....

b) Draw a line of best fit.

c) Use your graph to estimate ...

i) the time taken by John, who travelled a distance of 2.5 km.   ....

ii) the distance travelled by Donna, who takes 27 minutes. ....

2 The table below shows the heights and weights of 10 boys.

Height (cm)	133	162	130	163	153
Weight (kg)	70	84	64	87	87

Height (cm)	150	124	141	150	138
Weight (kg)	77	66	79	82	69

a) Use the information given to plot a scatter diagram, including line of best fit.

b) What type of correlation is there between height and weight?

....

c) i) Tony weighs 72kg. Use your graph to estimate his height. ....

ii) Rob is 1.57m tall. Use your graph to estimate his weight. ....

3 Mrs Thrift goes shopping at her local supermarket on 12 separate occasions. Each time she pays for her items with a £10 note. The table below shows the number of items bought and change received.

Change received (£)	2.50	5.60	5.70	7.80	0.90	3.10	5.20	4.20	1.50	7.90	6.80	2.70
Number of items bought	10	8	6	4	14	12	7	8	14	2	7	11

a) Use the information given to plot a scatter diagram including line of best fit.

b) What type of correlation does the scatter diagram show? ....

....

c) i) Mrs Thrift buys 9 items. Estimate how much change she receives. ....

ii) Mrs Thrift receives £6.20 in change. Estimate how many items she bought.

....

4 The table below shows the number of tracks and total playing time for 12 music CDs.

Number of tracks	14	20	8	11	18	14
Total time (mins)	62	69	58	61	66	67

Number of tracks	10	5	16	7	18	6
Total time (mins)	56	46	66	56	69	52

a) Use the information given to plot a scatter diagram including line of best fit.

b) i) If a CD has 13 tracks, estimate its total playing time. ....

ii) If the total playing time of a CD is 54 minutes, estimate the number of tracks it has. ....

5 The table gives information about the number of chapters and the total number of pages in books on Diane's shelf.

Number of chapters	19	28	11	14	27	23	8	16	21	25	32	19	35	11	16
Total number of pages	250	355	110	230	235	350	145	200	235	315	325	120	395	125	305

a) Use the information given to plot a scatter diagram including line of best fit.

b) What does the scatter diagram tell you about the relationship between the number of chapters and total number of pages?

c) Use your graph to estimate **i)** the total number of pages if a book has 24 chapters

ii) the number of chapters if a book has a total of 190 pages.

1 In one week a travel agent sold 120 separate holidays. The table below shows the holiday destinations.

Holiday Destination	No. of holidays sold
Spain	42
Greece	12
France	34
Cyprus	22
Italy	10

a) Draw and label a pie chart to represent these destinations.

b) What percentage of the holidays sold were for Spain?

....

c) What fraction of the holidays sold were for Greece?

....

2 Rose has completed 40 pieces of work in Maths in one school year. Her grades are as follows:

B, C, A, B, C, D, B, C, B, E, D,
A, B, C, D, B, C, B, B, D, A, C,
C, B, A, D, A, C, B, C, B, A, D,
E, C, B, C, C, B, D.

a) Draw a table to show the distribution of grades.

b) Draw and label a pie chart to show the distribution.

c) What fraction of Rose's grades were A's or B's?

....

Pie Charts (cont)

3 **60 men and 60 women were asked, 'What is your favourite colour of car?'**

The two pie charts show the results.

a) i) How many men chose red as their favourite colour?

....

ii) How many women chose red as their favourite colour?

....

b) Did more men or women choose green as their favourite colour? Show your working.

....

....

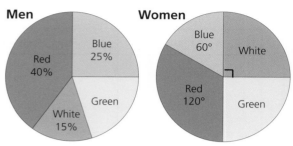

4 **This pie chart shows the daily newspaper bought by 72 people.**

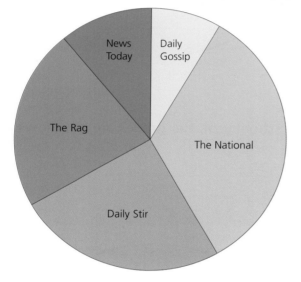

a) i) Which is the most popular newspaper?

....

ii) Which is the least popular newspaper?

....

b) i) How many people buy the Daily Stir?

....

....

ii) How many more people buy The National compared to News Today?

....

....

5 This table shows the number of telephone calls Mrs Chattergee makes in one week.

Day of the week	Monday	Tuesday	Wednesday	Thursday	Friday	Saturday	Sunday
Number of phone calls	3	2	8	4	7	10	6

a) Draw and label a pie chart to represent the information.
b) What percentage of the telephone calls were made at the weekend?

6 The ages of the people living in Addick Close are as follows:
2, 24, 14, 8, 70, 15, 19, 31, 85, 4, 3, 12, 30, 27, 45, 50, 66, 68, 2, 11,
74, 31, 63, 28, 41, 47, 51, 14, 18, 83, 69, 7, 52, 35, 33, 20, 14, 6, 7, 5.
a) Construct a frequency table to show the distribution of ages using class intervals of 1-20, 21-40, etc.
b) Draw and label a pie chart to show the distribution. c) What percentage of the residents are aged 41 or more?

7 A group of men and women were asked how they travel to work.
The two pie charts show their responses. They are not drawn accurately.
a) If 10 men travel to work by car, how many men
   travel to work by i) bus? ii) train?
b) If 20 women travel to work by train, how many women
   travel to work by i) car? ii) bus?

Mean, Median, Mode & Range 1

1 Laura has the following coins in her pocket:

Calculate the mean, median, mode and range for the coins.

Mean: ....

....

Median: .... Mode: .... Range: ....

2 The table below shows the results of an Internet search for the price of a particular camera.

Calculate the mean, mode, median and range of the camera prices.

Camera	Cost (£)	Camera	Cost (£)	Camera	Cost (£)	Camera	Cost (£)	Camera	Cost (£)
1	227	5	169	9	225	13	211	17	155
2	246	6	204	10	210	14	248	18	153
3	248	7	220	11	239	15	166	19	196
4	248	8	165	12	227	16	170	20	173

Mean: ....

....

Median: .... Mode: .... Range: ....

3 The weights of the 11 players in the Year 11 hockey team were measured.

Their weights in Kilograms were: 51, 60, 62, 47, 53, 48, 52, 51, 65, 61, 66

a) Calculate the mean, median, mode and range for their weights.

Mean: ....

....

Median: .... Mode: .... Range: ....

b) The weights of the 11 players in the Year 10 hockey team were also measured.

Their mean was 52.5kg and the range was 11kg. Compare the weights of the two teams.

....

....

4 9A contains 14 girls. Their heights in metres are:
1.46, 1.62, 1.57, 1.6, 1.39, 1.71, 1.53, 1.62, 1.58, 1.40, 1.46, 1.63, 1.62, 1.65
a) Calculate the mean, median, mode and range for the heights.
b) The boys in 9A have a mean height of 1.68m and a range of 0.32m. Compare the heights of the girls and the boys.

Mean, Median, Mode & Range 2

1 Janet carries out a survey on the number of passengers in cars which pass her house.

Here are the results:

Number of passengers	Frequency	Frequency x No. of passengers
0	11	
1	12	
2	6	
3	8	
4	3	

a) How many cars were there in her survey?....................

b) What is the modal number of passengers? ....

c) What is the median number of passengers? ....

d) What is the range of the number of passengers?

e) What is the mean number of passengers?

....

....

2 This graph shows the number of chocolate bars bought by pupils at a school tuck shop.

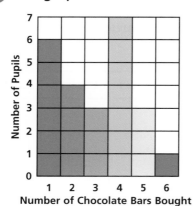

Number of Pupils

Number of Chocolate Bars Bought

a) How many pupils bought chocolate bars? ....

b) What is the modal number of bars bought? ....

c) What is the median number of bars bought? ....

d) What is the mean number of bars bought?

....

....

....

3 Phil carries out a survey about the amount of pocket money his classmates each receive every day. The results are shown below.

Amount of pocket money, (£)	Frequency		
0.50	3		
1.00	15		
1.50	8		
2.00	5		
2.50	1		

a) Calculate the mean amount of pocket money the pupils receive.

....

....

b) What is the median amount of pocket money received? ....

c) What is the modal amount of pocket money received?....................

4 The table below shows the number of goals scored by the Year 11 football team in one season.

Number of goals scored	0	1	2	3	4	5	6
Number of games	7	5	11	3	3	0	1

a) What is **i)** the mean **ii)** the range **iii)** the mode and **iv)** the median of the number of goals scored? **b)** The Year 10 football team averaged 2.2 goals per game in five less games. Which year scored the most goals and by how much?

Lonsdale Revision Guides

All you need for HIGHER TIER ...

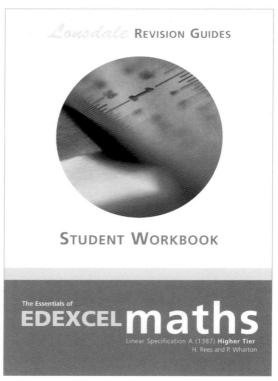

All you need for INTERMEDIATE TIER ...

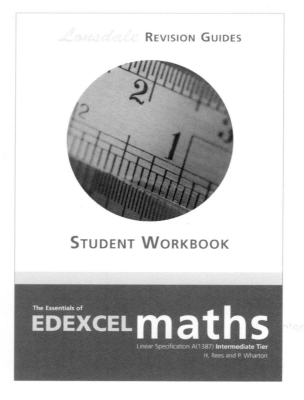

For ordering details see the inside front cover ...